The Power is Within You

BOOKS AND AUDIO TAPES BY LOUISE L. HAY

Books

The AIDS Book: Creating A Positive Approach
Colors & Numbers
Heal Your Body
Heart Thoughts: A Treasury of Inner Wisdom
A Garden of Thoughts: My Affirmation Journal
Love Your Body
Love Yourself, Heal Your Life Workbook
You Can Heal Your Life

Audio Tapes

AIDS: A Positive Approach
Cancer: Discovering Your Healing Power
Feeling Fine Affirmations
Gift of the Present with Joshua Leeds
Heal Your Body Book on Tape
Love Your Body Book on Tape
Loving Yourself
Morning and Evening Meditations
Self Healing
Songs of Affirmation with Joshua Leeds
What I Believe/Deep Relaxation
You Can Heal Your Life Study Course
You Can Heal Your Life Book on Tape

Conversations on Living Lecture Series

Change and Transition
Dissolving Barriers
The Forgotten Child Within
How to Love Yourself
The Power of Your Spoken Word
Receiving Prosperity
Totality of Possibilities
Your Thoughts Create Your Life

Personal Power Through Imagery Series

Anger Releasing
Forgiveness/Loving the Inner Child

Subliminal Mastery Series

Feeling Fine Affirmations
Love Your Body Affirmations
Safe Driving Affirmations
Self-Esteem Affirmations
Self-Healing Affirmations
Stress-Free Affirmations

Louise L. Hay

The Power is Within You

with Linda Carwin Tomchin

Hay House, Inc.
Carson, CA

THE POWER IS WITHIN YOU
by Louise L. Hay

Copyright © 1991 by Louise L. Hay

Library of Congress Cataloging-in-Publication Data

Hay, Louise L.
  The power is within you / Louise L. Hay with Linda Carwin Tomchin.
    p. cm.
  Includes bibliographical references.
  ISBN 1-56170-019-3 : $18.00. — ISBN 1-56170-023-1 (pbk.)
  1. Self-acceptance.   2. Change (Psychology)   I. Tomchin, Linda
Carwin, 1947–   . II. Title.
BF575.S37H4   1991   91-71179
155.2—dc20   CIP

Library of Congress Catalog Card No. 91-71179
ISBN: 1-56170-019-3

Internal design by David Butler
Typesetting by Freedmen's Organization, Los Angeles, CA 90004

91 92 93 94 95 96   10 9 8 7 6 5 4 3 2
Second printing, August 1991

Published and Distributed in the United States by

Hay House, Inc.
1154 E. Dominguez St.
Post Office Box 6204
Carson, CA 90749-6204 USA

Printed in the United States of America

Dedication

I lovingly dedicate this book to all those who have at-
tended my workshops and trainings, the teachers of my
workshops, my staff at Hay House, those powerful people at the *Hayride*, all the wonderful people who have
written me over the years, and to Linda Carwin Tomchin,
whose help and input into the creation of this book was
indispensable. My heart has grown so much in knowing
each and every one of you.

Table of Contents

PART FIVE
LETTING GO OF THE PAST

Foreword

There is a great deal of information in this book. Do not feel you have to absorb it all at once. Certain ideas will leap out at you. Work with those ideas first. If I say anything that you disagree with, just ignore it. If you can get just one good idea out of this book and use it to improve the quality of your life, then I feel complete in writing it.

As you read you will become aware that I use many terms such as *Power, Intelligence, Infinite Mind, Higher Power, God, Universal Power, Inner Wisdom* . . . and so on. This is done to show you that there is no limitation on what you choose to call that Power that runs the Universe and is also within you. If any name disturbs you, then substitute another that feels right for you. In the past I have even crossed out words or names that did not appeal to me when I read a book and wrote in the word that I liked better. You could do the same.

You will also notice that I spell two words differently than they are normally spelled. *Disease* is spelled *dis-ease* and denotes anything that is not in harmony with you or your environment. *AIDS* is spelled in lower-case letters—*aids*—to diminish the power of the word, and therefore, the dis-ease. This idea was originally created by the Reverend Stephan Pieters. We at Hay House heartily endorse this concept, and urge our readers to do so as well.

This book was written as an extension of *You Can Heal Your Life*. Time has passed since the writing of that book and many new ideas have revealed themselves to me. Those ideas I wish to share with all of you who have been writing over the years asking for more information. I feel an important thing to be aware of is that the Power we are all seeking "out there" is also within us and readily available to us to use in positive ways. May this book reveal to you how very powerful you really are.

Introduction

I am not a healer. I do not heal anyone. I think of myself as a stepping stone on a pathway of self-discovery. I create a space where people can learn how incredibly wonderful they are by teaching them to love themselves. That's all I do. I'm a person who supports people. I help people take charge of their lives. I help them discover their own power and inner wisdom and strengths. I help them get the blocks and the barriers out of the way, so they can love themselves no matter what circumstances they happen to be going through. This doesn't mean that we will never have problems, but it is how we react to the problem that makes a tremendous difference.

After years of individual counseling with clients and conducting hundreds of workshops and intensive training programs across the country and around the world, I found that there is only one thing that heals every problem, and that is: *to love yourself*. When people start to love themselves more each day, it's amazing how their lives get better. They feel better. They get the jobs they want. They have the money they need. Their relationships either improve, or the negative ones dissolve and new ones begin. It's a very simple premise—*loving yourself*. I've been criticized for being too simplistic, and I have found that the simple things are usually the most profound.

Someone said to me recently, "You gave me the most wonderful gift—you gave me the gift of myself." So many of us hide from ourselves and we don't even know who we are. We don't know what we feel, we don't know what we want. Life is a voyage of self discovery. To me, to be enlightened is to go within and to know who and what we really are, and to know that we have the ability to change for the better by loving and taking care of ourselves. It's not selfish to love ourselves. It clears us so that we can love ourselves enough to love other people. We can really help the planet when we come from a space of great love and joy on an individual basis.

The Power that created this incredible Universe has often been referred to as *love. God is love.* We have often heard the statement: *Love makes the world go 'round.* It's all true. Love is the binding agent that holds the whole Universe together.

To me, love is a deep appreciation. When I talk about loving ourselves, I mean having a deep appreciation for who we are. We accept all the different parts of ourselves—our little peculiarities, the embarrassments, the things we may not do so well, and all the wonderful qualities, too. We accept the whole package with love. Unconditionally.

Unfortunately, many of us will not love ourselves until we lose the weight, or get the job, or get the raise, or the boyfriend, or whatever. We often put conditions on our love. But we can change. We *can* love ourselves as we are right now!

There is also a lack of love on this planet as a whole. I believe our whole planet has a dis-ease called aids, and more and more people are dying every day. This physical challenge has given us the opportunity to overcome barriers and go beyond our morality standards and differences of religion and politics and to open our hearts. The more of us who can do it, the quicker we are going to find the answers.

We are in the midst of enormous individual and global change. I believe that all of us who are living at this time chose to be here to be a part of these changes, to bring about change, and to transform the world from the old way of life to a more loving and peaceful existence. In the Piscean Age we looked "out there" for our savior: "Save me. Save me. Please take care of me." Now we are moving into the Aquarian Age, and we are learning to go within to find our savior. We are the power we have been seeking. We are in charge of our lives.

If you are not willing to love yourself today, then you are not going to love yourself tomorrow, because whatever excuse you have today, you'll still have tomorrow. Maybe you'll have the same excuse 20 years from now, and even leave this lifetime holding on to the same excuse. Today is the day you can love yourself totally with no expectations.

I want to help create a world where it is safe for us to love each other, where we can express who we are and be loved and accepted by the people around us without judgment, criticism, or prejudice. Loving begins at home. The bible says, *"Love thy neighbor as thyself."* Far too often we forget the last couple of words—*as thyself.* We really can't love anyone out there unless the love starts inside us. Self-love is the most important gift we can give ourselves, because when we love who we are, we will not hurt ourselves, and we will not hurt anyone else. With inner peace, there would be no wars, no gangs, no terrorists, and no homeless. There would be no dis-ease, no aids, no cancer, no poverty, and no starvation. So this, to me, is a prescription for world peace: *to have peace within ourselves*. Peace, understanding, compassion, forgiveness, and most of all, love. We have the power within us to effect these changes.

Love is something we can choose, the same way we choose anger, or hate, or sadness. We *can* choose love. It's always a choice within us. Let's begin right now in this moment to choose love. It's the most powerful healing force there is.

The information in this book, which has been a part of my lectures over the past five years, is yet another stepping stone on your pathway to self-discovery—an opportunity to know a little bit more about yourself and to understand the potential that is your birthright. You have an opportunity to love yourself more, so you can be a part of an incredible universe of love. Love begins in our hearts, and it begins with us. Let your love contribute to the healing of our planet.

Louise L. Hay
January 1991

PART ONE

Becoming Conscious

When we expand our thinking and beliefs, our love flows freely. When we contract, we shut ourselves off.

Chapter 1

The Power Within

*The more you connect to the Power
within you, the more you can be free
in all areas of your life.*

Who are you? Why are you here? What are your beliefs
about life? For thousands of years, finding the answers to
these questions has meant *going within*. But what does
that mean?

I believe there is a Power within each of us that can lovingly direct us to our perfect health, perfect relationships,
perfect careers, and which can bring us prosperity of every kind. In order to have these things, we have to believe
first that they are possible. Next, we must be willing to
release the patterns in our lives that are creating conditions we say we do not want. We do this by going within
and tapping the Inner Power that already knows what is
best for us. If we are willing to turn our lives over to this
greater Power within us, the Power that loves and sustains
us, we can create more loving and prosperous lives.

I believe that our minds are always connected to the
One Infinite Mind, and therefore, all knowledge and wisdom is available to us at any time. We are connected to

this Infinite Mind, this Universal Power that created us, through that spark of light within, our Higher Self, or the Power within. The Universal Power loves all of Its creations. It is a Power for good and It directs everything in our lives. It doesn't know how to hate or lie or punish. It is pure love, freedom, understanding, and compassion. It is important to turn our lives over to our Higher Self, because through It we receive our good.

We must understand that we have the choice to use this Power in any way. If we choose to live in the past and re-hash all of the negative situations and conditions that went on way back when, then we stay stuck where we are. If we make a conscious decision not to be victims of the past and go about creating new lives for ourselves, we are supported by this Power within, and new, happier experiences begin to unfold. I don't believe in two powers. I think there is One Infinite Spirit. It's all too easy to say, "It's the devil," or *them*. It really is only us, and either we use the power we have wisely or we misuse the power. Do we have the devil in our hearts? Do we condemn others for being different than we are? What are we choosing?

Responsibility Vs. Blame

I also believe that we contribute toward the creation of every condition in our lives, good or bad, with our thinking, feeling patterns. The thoughts we think create our feelings, and we then begin to live our lives in accordance with these feelings and beliefs. This is not to blame ourselves for things going *wrong* in our lives. There is a difference between being responsible and blaming ourselves or others.

When I talk about responsibility, I am really talking about having power. Blame is about giving away one's power. Responsibility gives us the power to make changes in our lives. If we play the victim role, then we are using our personal power to be helpless. If we decide to accept responsibility, then we don't waste time blaming somebody or something *out there*. Some people feel guilty for creating illness, or poverty, or problems. They choose to interpret responsibility as guilt. (Some members of the media like to refer to it as *New Age Guilt*.) These people feel guilty because they believe that they have failed in some way. However, they usually accept everything as a guilt trip in one way or another because it's another way to make themselves wrong. That is not what I'm talking about.

If we can use our problems and illnesses as opportunities to think about how we can change our lives, we have power. Many people who come through catastrophic illness say that it was the most wonderful thing that ever happened to them because it gave them a chance to go about their lives differently. A lot of people, on the other hand, go around saying, "I'm a victim, woe is me. Please, doctor, fix me." I think these people will have a difficult time even getting well or handling their problems.

Responsibility is our ability to respond to a situation. We always have a choice. It does not mean that we deny who we are and what we have in our lives. It merely means that we can acknowledge that we have contributed to where we are. By taking responsibility, we have the power to change. We can say, "What can I do to make this different?" We need to understand that we all have personal power *all the time*. It depends on how we use it.

Many of us are now realizing that we come from dysfunctional homes. We carry over a lot of negative feelings about who we are and our relationship to life. My childhood was filled with violence, including sexual abuse. I was starved for love and affection and had no self-esteem at all. Even after leaving home at the age of 15, I continued to experience abuse in many forms. I hadn't yet realized that the thinking, feeling patterns I had learned early in life had brought this abuse upon me.

Children often respond to the mental atmosphere of the adults around them. So I learned early about fear and abuse and continued to recreate those experiences for myself as I grew up. I certainly didn't understand that I had the power to change all of this. I was unmercifully hard on myself because I interpreted lack of love and affection to mean I must be a bad person.

All of the events you have experienced in your lifetime up to this moment have been created by your thoughts and beliefs from the past. Let's not look back on our lives with shame. Look at the past as part of the richness and fullness of your life. Without this richness and fullness, we would not be here today. There is no reason to beat yourself up because you didn't do better. You did the best you knew how. Release the past in love, and be grateful that it has brought you to this new awareness.

The past only exists in our minds and in the way we choose to look at it in our minds. *This* is the moment we are living. *This* is the moment we are feeling. *This* is the moment we are experiencing. What we are doing right now is laying the groundwork for tomorrow. So *this* is the moment to make the decision. We can't do anything tomorrow, and we can't do it yesterday. We can only do it today. What is important is what we are choosing to think, believe, and say *right now.*

When we begin to take conscious charge of our thoughts and words, then we have tools that we can use. I know this sounds simple, but remember, *the point of power is always in the present moment.*

It is important for you to understand that your mind is not in control. *You* are in control of your mind. The Higher Self is in control. You can stop thinking those old thoughts. When your old thinking tries to come back and say, "It's so hard to change," take mental command. Say to your mind, "I now choose to believe it is becoming easy for me to make changes." You may have this conversation with your mind several times before it acknowledges that you are in charge and that you really mean what you say.

Imagine that your thoughts are like drops of water. One thought or one drop of water does not mean very much. As you repeat thoughts over and over, you first notice a stain on the carpet, then there is a little puddle, then a pond, and as these thoughts continue, they can become a lake, and finally an ocean. What kind of ocean are you creating? One that is polluted and toxic and unfit to swim in, or one that is crystal clear and blue and invites you to enjoy its refreshing waters?

People often tell me, "I can't stop thinking a thought." I always reply, "Yes, you can." Remember, how often have you refused to think a positive thought? You just have to tell your mind that that is what you are going to do. You have to make up your mind to stop thinking negatively. I'm not saying that you have to fight your thoughts when you want to change things. When the negative thoughts come up, simply say, "Thank you for sharing." In that way, you are not denying what is there, and you are not giving your power over to the negative thought. Tell yourself that you are not going to buy into the negativity anymore. You want to create another way of thinking. Again, you don't have to fight your thoughts. Acknowledge and go beyond them. Don't drown in a sea of your own negativity, when you can float on the ocean of life.

You are meant to be a wonderful, loving expression of life. Life is waiting for you to open up to it—to feel worthy of the good it holds for you. The wisdom and intelligence of the Universe is yours to use. Life is here to support you. Trust the Power within you to be there for you.

If you get scared, it is helpful to become aware of your breath as it flows in and out of your body. Your breath, the most precious substance of your life, is freely given to you. You have enough to last for as long as you live. You accept this precious substance without even thinking, and yet you doubt that life can supply you with the other necessities. Now is the time for you to learn about your own power and what you are capable of doing. Go within and find out who you are.

We all have different opinions. You have a right to yours and I have a right to mine. No matter what goes on in the world, the only thing you can work on is what is right for you. You have to get in touch with your inner guidance because it is the wisdom that knows the answers for you. It's not easy to listen to yourself when your friends and family are telling you what to do. Yet, all the answers to all the questions you are ever going to ask are within you now.

Every time you say, "I don't know," you shut the door to your own inner wisdom. The messages you get from your Higher Self are positive and supportive of you. If you start getting negative messages, then you are working from ego and your human mind level, and even perhaps your imagination, although positive messages often come to us through our imagination and our dreams.

Support yourself by making the right choices for you. When in doubt, ask yourself, *"Is this a decision that is loving for me? Is this right for me now?'* You may make another decision at some later point, a day, a week, or a month later. But ask yourself these questions in each moment.

As we learn to love ourselves and trust our Higher Power, we become co-creators with the Infinite Spirit of a loving world. Our love for ourselves moves us from being victims to being winners. Our love for ourselves attracts wonderful experiences to us. Have you ever noticed that people who feel good about themselves are naturally attractive? They usually have a quality about them that is just wonderful. They are happy with their lives. Things come to them easily and effortlessly.

I learned a long time ago that I am a being of oneness with the Presence and Power of God. Knowing this, that the wisdom and understanding of Spirit resides within me, and I am, therefore, divinely guided in all my dealings with others upon the planet. Just as all the stars and planets are in their perfect orbit, I am also in my divine right order. I may not understand everything with my limited human mind; however, on the cosmic level, I know I am in the right place, at the right time, doing the right thing. My present experience is a stepping stone to new awareness and new opportunities.

Who are you? What did you come here to learn? What did you come here to teach? We all have a unique purpose. We are more than our personalities, our problems, our fears, and our illnesses. We are far more than our bodies. We are all connected with everyone on the planet and with all of life. We are all spirit, light, energy, vibration, and love, and we all have the power to live our lives with purpose and meaning.

Chapter 2

Following My Inner Voice

*The thoughts we choose to think are
the tools we use to paint the canvas of
our lives.*

I remember when I first heard that I could change my life
if I was willing to change my thinking. It was quite a
revolutionary idea to me. I lived in New York and discovered the Church of Religious Science. (Often people
confuse the Church of Religious Science, or Science of
Mind, which was founded by Ernest Holmes, with the
Christian Science Church founded by Mary Baker Eddy.
They all reflect *new thought*; however, they are different
philosophies.)

The Science of Mind has ministers and practitioners
who carry on the teachings of the Church of Religious
Science (the Church). They were the very first people who
told me that my thoughts shaped my future. Even though
I didn't understand what they meant, this concept
touched what I call the *inner ding* within me, that place
of intuition that is referred to as the *voice within*. Over
the years, I've learned to follow it, because when that *ding*
goes "Yes," even if it seems a crazy choice, I know that
it's right for me.

So these concepts struck a cord in me. Something said, "Yes, they are right." And then I began the adventure of learning how to change my thinking. Once I accepted the idea and said "yes" to it, I went through the hows. I read a lot of books, and my home became like many of yours, filled with masses of spiritual and self-help books. I went to classes for many years, and I explored everything related to the subject. I literally immersed myself in *new thought* philosophy. It was the first time that I had really studied in my life. Up until then I didn't believe in anything. My mother was a lapsed Catholic, and my stepfather was an atheist. I had some strange idea that Christians either wore hair shirts or were eaten by lions, and neither appealed to me.

I really delved into the Science of Mind, because that was an avenue that was open for me at the time, and I found it really wonderful. At first it was sort of easy. I grasped a few concepts, and I started to think and talk a little bit differently. In those days I was a constant complainer and full of self-pity. I just loved to wallow in the pits. I didn't know that I was continually perpetuating more experiences in which to pity myself. But then again, I didn't know any better in those days. Gradually, I found that I was no longer complaining quite so much.

I started to listen to what I said. I became aware of my self-criticism, and I tried to stop it. I began to babble affirmations without quite knowing what they meant. I started with the easy ones, of course, and a few small changes began to take place. I got the green lights and the parking places, and boy, did I think I was hot stuff. Oh wow! I thought I knew it all, and I very soon became quite cocky and arrogant and dogmatic in my beliefs. I felt I knew all the answers. In hindsight, it was really my way of feeling safe in this new area.

When we start to move away from some of our old rigid beliefs, especially if we've previously been in total control, it can be very scary. It was very frightening for me, so I would grasp onto whatever would make me feel safe. It was a beginning for me, and I still had a long way to go. And still do.

Like most of us, I didn't always find the pathway easy and smooth because just babbling affirmations didn't work all the time, and I couldn't understand why. I asked myself, "What am I doing wrong?" Immediately, I blamed myself. Was this one more example of me not being good enough? That was a favorite old belief of mine.

At the time my teacher, Eric Pace, would look at me and refer to the idea of *resentment*. I didn't have the faintest idea what he was talking about. Resentment? Me? Surely, I didn't have any resentments. After all, I was on my pathway, I was spiritually perfect. How little I could see myself then!

I continued doing the best I could in my life. I studied metaphysics and spirituality and learned about myself as much as possible. I grasped what I could, and sometimes, I applied it. Often, we hear a lot of things, and sometimes we grasp them, but we don't always practice them. Time seemed to go by very quickly, and at that point, I had been studying Science of Mind for about three years and had become a practitioner of the Church. I began to teach the philosophy, but I wondered why my students seemed to be floundering. I couldn't understand why they were so stuck in their problems. I gave them so much good advice. Why weren't they using it and getting well? It never dawned on me that I was speaking the truth more than I was living it. I was like a parent who tells the child what to do but then does exactly the opposite.

Then one day, seemingly out of the blue, I was diagnosed with vaginal cancer. First, I panicked. Then, I had doubts that all this stuff I was learning was valid. It was a normal and natural reaction. I thought to myself, "If I was clear and centered, I wouldn't have the need to create the illness." In hindsight, I think when I was diagnosed, I felt safe enough at that point to let the illness surface so that I could do something about it, rather than having it be another hidden secret that I wouldn't know about until I was dead.

I knew too much by then to hide from myself any longer. I knew that cancer was a dis-ease of resentment that is held for a long time until it eats away at the body. When we stifle our emotions inside of us, they have to go somewhere in the body. If we spend a lifetime stuffing things down, they will eventually manifest somewhere in the body.

I became very aware that the resentment (which my teacher had referred to so many times) within me had to do with being physically, emotionally, and sexually abused as a child. Naturally, I would have resentment. I was bitter and unforgiving of the past. I had never done any work to change or release the bitterness and let it go. When I left home, it was all I could do to forget what happened to me; I thought I had put it behind me when in actuality I had simply buried it.

When I found my metaphysical pathway, I covered up my feelings with a nice layer of spirituality and hid a lot of garbage inside me. I put a wall around myself that kept me literally out of touch with my own feelings. I didn't know who I was or where I was. After my diagnosis, the real inner work of learning to know myself began. Thank God, I had tools to use. I knew I needed to go within myself if I was going to make any permanent changes. Yes, the doctor could give me an operation and perhaps take care of my illness for the moment, but if I didn't change the way I was using my thoughts and my words, I'd probably re-create it again.

It is always interesting to me to learn where in our bodies we put our cancers—on which side of the body are our tumors, the left or the right. The right side represents the masculine side, from where we give out. The left is the feminine side, the receptive part, from where we take in. Almost all of my life, when anything went wrong, it was always on the right side of my body. It was where I stored all the resentment toward my stepfather.

I was no longer content to get green lights and parking places. I knew that I had to go much, much deeper. I realized that I was not really progressing in my life the way

I wanted to because I hadn't really cleared out this old garbage from childhood, and I wasn't living what I was teaching. I had to recognize the inner child inside me and work with her. My inner child needed help because she was still in great pain.

I quickly began a self-healing program in earnest. I concentrated on *me* totally and did little else. I became very committed to getting well. Some of it was a little weird, yet I did it anyway. After all, this was my life on the line. It became almost a 24-hour-a-day job for the next six months. I began reading and studying everything I could find about alternative ways to heal cancer because I truly believed it could be done. I did a nutritional cleansing program that detoxified my body from all the junk foods I had eaten for years. For months, I seemed to be living on sprouts and pureed asparagus. I know I had more to eat, but that is what I remember the most.

I worked with my Science of Mind practitioner and teacher, Eric Pace, to clear the mental patterns so the cancer wouldn't return. I said affirmations and did visualizations and spiritual mind treatments. I did daily sessions in front of a mirror. The most difficult words to say were, "I love you, I really love you." It took a lot of tears and a lot of breathing to get through it. When I did, it was as if I took a quantum leap. I went to a good psychotherapist who was skilled in helping people express and release their anger. I spent a long period of time beating pillows and screaming. It was wonderful. It felt so good because I had never, ever had permission to do that in my life.

I don't know which method worked; maybe a little bit

of everything worked. Most of all I was really consistent with what I did. I practiced during all my waking hours. I thanked myself before I went to sleep for what I had done during the day. I affirmed that my healing process was taking place in my body while I slept, and that I would awaken in the morning bright and refreshed and feeling good. In the morning, I'd awaken and thank myself and my body for the work during the night. I would affirm that I was willing to grow and learn each day and make changes without seeing myself as a bad person.

I also worked on understanding and forgiveness. One of the ways was to explore my parents' childhoods as much as I could. I began to understand how they were treated as children, and I realized that because of the way they were brought up, they couldn't really have done anything differently than they did. My stepfather was abused at home, and he continued this abuse with his children. My mother was brought up to believe the man was always right and you stood by and let him do what he wanted. No one taught them a different approach. It was their way of life. Step by step, my growing understanding of them enabled me to start the forgiveness process.

The more I forgave my parents, the more willing I was to forgive myself. Forgiveness of ourselves is enormously important. Many of us do the same damage to the inner child that our parents did to us. We just continue the abuse, and it's very sad. When we were children and other people mistreated us, we didn't have many options, but when we grow up and we *still* mistreat the inner child, it's disastrous.

As I forgave myself, I began to trust myself. I found

that when we don't trust life or other people, it's really be-cause we don't trust ourselves. We don't trust our Higher Selves to take care of us in all situations, so we say, "I'll never fall in love again because I don't want to get hurt," or "I'll never let this happen again." What we are really saying to ourselves is, "I don't trust you enough to take good care of me, so I'm going to stay away from everything."

Eventually, I began to trust myself enough to take care of me, and I found it easier and easier to love myself once I trusted myself. My body was healing, and my heart was healing.

My spiritual growth had come in such an unexpected way.

As a bonus, I began to look younger. The clients I now attracted were almost all people who were willing to work on themselves. They made enormous progress without me really saying anything. They could sense and feel that I was living the concepts I was teaching, and it was easy for them to accept these ideas. Of course, they had positive results. They began to improve the quality of their lives. Once we begin to make peace with ourselves on the in-ner level, life seems to flow much more pleasantly.

So what did this experience teach me personally? I real-ized that I had the power to change my life if I was will-ing to change my thinking and release the patterns that kept me living in the past. This experience gave me the inner knowledge that if we are really willing to do the work, we can make incredible changes in our minds, our bodies, and our lives.

No matter where you are in life, no matter what you've contributed to creating, no matter what's happening, you are always doing the best you can with the understanding and awareness and knowledge that you have. And when you know more, you will do it differently, as I did. Don't berate yourself for where you are. Don't blame yourself for not doing it faster or better. Say to yourself, "I'm doing the best I can, and even though I'm in a pickle now, I will get out of it somehow, so let's find the best way to do it." If all you do is tell yourself that you're stupid and no good, then you stay stuck. You need your own loving support if you want to make changes.

The methods I use are not my methods. Most of them I learned at Science of Mind, which is what I basically teach. Yet these principles are as old as time. If you read any of the old spiritual teachings you will find the same messages. I am trained as a minister of the Church of Religious Science; however, I do not have a church. I am a free spirit. I express the teachings in simple language so that they reach many people. This path is a wonderful way of getting your head together and really understanding what life is all about, and how you can use your mind to take charge of your life. When I started all this 20 or so years ago, I had no idea that I would be able to bring hope and help to the number of people that I do today.

Chapter 3

The Power of Your Spoken Word

*Every day declare for yourself what
you want in life. Declare it as though
you have it!*

The Law of Mind

There is a law of gravity, and there are several other physical laws, like physics and electricity, most of which I don't understand. There are also spiritual laws, like the law of cause and effect: *what you give out comes back.* There is also a law of mind. I don't know how it works, in much the same way that I don't know how electricity works. I only know that when I flick the switch, the light comes on.

 I believe that when we think a thought or when we speak a word or sentence, it somehow goes out from us into a law of mind and comes back to us as experience.

We are now beginning to learn the correlation between the mental and the physical. We are beginning to understand how the mind works and that our thoughts are creative. Our thoughts speed through our minds very quickly, so it is difficult to shape them at first. Our mouths, on the

21

other hand, are slower. So if we can start editing our speech by listening to what we say and not letting negative things come out of our mouths, then we can begin to shape our thoughts.

There is tremendous power in our spoken words, and many of us are not aware just how important they are. Let us consider words as the foundation of what we continually create in our lives. We use words all the time, yet we babble away, seldom thinking about what we are truly saying or how we are saying it. We pay very little attention to the selection of our words. In fact, most of us speak in negatives.

As children we were taught grammar. We were taught to select words according to these rules of grammar. However, I have always found that the rules of grammar continually change, and what was improper at one time is proper at another time, or vice versa. What was slang in the past is considered common usage in the present. However, grammar does not take into consideration the meaning of words and how they affect our lives.

 On the other hand, I was not taught in school that my choice of words would have anything to do with what I would experience in life. No one taught me that my thoughts were creative, or that they could literally shape my life. Nobody taught me that what I gave out in the form of words would return to me as experiences. The purpose of the golden rule was to show us a very basic law of life: *"Do unto others as you would do unto yourself."* What you give out comes back to you. It was never meant to cause guilt. No one ever taught me that I was worth loving or that I deserved good. And nobody taught me that life was here to support me.

I remember that as children, we would often call each other cruel and hurtful names and try to belittle one another. But why did we? Where did we learn such behavior? Look at what we were taught. Many of us were told repeatedly by our parents that we were stupid or dumb or lazy. We were a nuisance and not good enough. Sometimes we heard our parents say that they wished we had never been born. Maybe we cringed when we heard these words, but little did we realize how deeply imbedded the hurt and pain would become.

Changing Our Self-Talk

Too often, we accepted the early messages that our parents gave us. We heard, "Eat your spinach," "Clean your room," or "Make your bed," in order to be loved. You got the idea that you were only acceptable if you did certain things—that acceptance and love were conditional. However, that was according to somebody's idea of what was worthwhile and had nothing to do with your deep, inner self-worth. You got the idea that you could only exist if you did these things to please others, otherwise you did not have permission to even exist.

These early messages contribute to what I call our *self-talk*—the way we talk to ourselves. The way we talk to ourselves inwardly is really important because it becomes the basis of our spoken words. It sets up the mental atmosphere in which we operate and which attracts to us our experiences. If we belittle ourselves, life is going to *post* mean very little to us. If we love and appreciate ourselves, then life can be a wonderful, joyous gift.

If our lives are unhappy, or if we are feeling unfulfilled, it's very easy to blame our parents, or *them*, and say it's all *their* fault. However, if we do, we stay stuck in our conditions, our problems, and our frustrations. Words of blame will not bring us freedom. Remember, there is power in our words. Again, our power comes from taking responsibility for our lives. I know it sounds scary to be responsible for our lives, but we really are, whether we accept it or not. If we want to be responsible for our lives, we've got to be responsible for our mouths. The words and phrases we say are extensions of our thoughts.

Start to listen to what you say. If you hear yourself using negative or limiting words, change them. If I hear a negative story, I don't go around repeating it to everyone. I think it has gone far enough, and I let it go. If I hear a positive story, however, I will tell everyone.

When you are out with other people, begin to listen to what they say and how they say it. See if you can connect what they say with what they are experiencing in life. Many, many people live their lives in *shoulds*. *Should* is a word that my ear is very attuned to. It is as if a bell goes off every time I hear it. Often, I will hear people use a dozen *shoulds* in a paragraph. These same people wonder why their lives are so rigid or why they can't move out of a situation. They want a lot of control over things that they cannot control. They are either making themselves wrong or making someone else wrong. And then they question why they aren't living lives of freedom.

We can also remove the expression _have to_ from our vocabulary and our thinking as well. When we do, we will release a lot of self-imposed pressure on ourselves. We create tremendous pressure by saying, "I have to go to work. I have to do this. I have to . . . I have to . . . "Instead, let's begin to say, _choose to._ "I choose to go to work because it pays the rent right now." _Choose to_ puts a whole different perspective on our lives. Everything we do is by choice even though it may not seem to be so.

A lot of us also use the word _but._ We make statements, then we say _but,_ which heads us in two different directions. We give conflicting messages to ourselves. Listen to how you use the word _but_ the next time you speak.

Another expression we need to be mindful of is _don't forget._ We're so used to saying, "Don't forget this or that," and what happens? We forget. We really want to remember and instead we forget, so we can begin to use the phrase _please remember_ in place of _don't forget._

When you wake up in the morning, do you curse the fact that you have to go to work? Do you complain about the weather? Do you grumble that your back or head hurts? What is the second thing and the third thing you think or say? Do you yell at the children to get up? Most people say more or less the same thing every morning. How does what you say start your day? Is it positive and cheerful and wonderful? Or is it whining and condemning? If you grumble and complain and moan, you're setting yourself up for such a day.

What are your last thoughts before going to bed? Are they powerful healing thoughts or poverty worry thoughts? When I speak of poverty thoughts, I don't only mean about the lack of money. It can be a negative way of thinking about anything in your life—any part of your life that is not flowing freely. Do you worry about tomorrow? Usually, I will read something positive before I go to sleep. I am aware that when I sleep I am doing a lot of clearing that will prepare me for the next day.

I find it very helpful to turn over to my dreams any problems or questions I may have. I know my dreams will help me take care of whatever is going on in my life.

I am the only person who can think in my mind, just like you are the only person who can think in your mind. Nobody can force us to think in a different way. We choose our thoughts, and these are the basis for our *self-talk*. As I experienced how this process worked more in my life, I began to live more of what I was teaching others. I really watched my words and my thoughts, and I constantly forgave myself for not being perfect. I allowed myself to be me, rather than struggling to be a super person who may only be acceptable in others' eyes.

When I began for the first time to trust life and to see it as a friendly place, I lightened up. My humor became less biting and more truly funny. I worked on releasing criticism and judgment of myself and other people, and I stopped telling disaster stories. We are so quick to spread bad news. It's just amazing. I stopped reading the newspaper and gave up the 11 o'clock news at night, because all the reports were concerned with disaster and violence and very little good news. I realized that most people don't want to hear good news. They love to hear bad news, so they have something to complain about. Too many of us keep recycling the negative stories until we believe that there is only bad in the world. For awhile there was a radio station that broadcast only good news. It went out of business.

When I had my cancer, I decided to stop gossiping, and to my surprise, I found I had nothing to say to anyone. I became aware that whenever I met a friend, I would immediately dish the latest dirt with them. Eventually, I discovered there were other ways of talking, although it wasn't an easy habit to break. Nonetheless, if I gossiped about other people, then other people probably gossiped about me, because what we give out we get back.

As I worked more and more with people, I really began to listen to what they said. I really began to hear the words, not just get the general drift. Usually, after ten minutes with a new client, I could tell exactly why they had a problem because I could hear the words they were using. I could understand them by the way they were talking. I knew that their words were contributing to their problems. If they were talking negatively, imagine what their *self-talk* was like? It must be more of the same negative programming—poverty thinking—as I called it.

A little exercise I suggest you do is to put a tape recorder by your telephone, and every time you make or get a call, push the record button. When the tape is full on both sides, listen to what you have been saying and how you say it. You will probably be amazed. You will begin to hear the words you use and the inflection of your voice. You will begin to become aware. If you find yourself saying something three times or more, write it down because it is a pattern. Some of the patterns may be positive and supportive, and you also may have some very negative patterns that you repeat over and over and over again.

The Power of the Subconscious Mind

In light of what I've been speaking of, I want to discuss the power of our subconscious minds. Our subconscious minds make no judgments. The subconscious mind accepts everything we say and creates according to our beliefs. It always says *yes*. Our subconscious minds love us enough to give us what we declare. We have choice, though. If we choose these poverty beliefs and concepts, then it is assumed that we want them. It will continue to give us these things until we are willing to change our thoughts and words and beliefs for the better. We are never stuck because we can always choose again. There are billions and billions of thoughts from which to choose.

Our subconscious minds don't know true from false or right from wrong. We don't want to deprecate ourselves in any way. We don't want to say something like, "Oh stupid, old me," because the subconscious mind will pick this *self-talk* up, and after a while you will feel that way.

If you say it enough times, it will become a belief in your subconscious.

The subconscious mind has no sense of humor, and it is important for you to know and understand this concept. You cannot make a joke about yourself and think it doesn't mean anything. If it is a put-down about yourself, even if you are trying to be cute or funny about it, the subconscious mind accepts it as true. I don't let people tell put-down jokes in my workshops. They can be raunchy but not put-downs of a nationality or sex or whatever.

So don't joke about yourself and make derogatory remarks about yourself because they will not create good experiences for you. Don't belittle others either. The subconscious mind doesn't distinguish between you and the other person. It hears the words, and it believes you are talking about yourself. The next time you want to criticize someone, ask why you feel that way about yourself. You only see in others what you see in yourself. Instead of criticizing others, praise them, and within a month, you will see enormous change within you.

Our words are really a matter of approach and attitude. Notice the way that lonely, unhappy, poor, sick people talk. What words do they use? What have they accepted as the truth for themselves? How do they describe themselves? How do they describe their work, their lives, their relationships? What do they look forward to? Be aware of their words, but please don't run around telling strangers that they are ruining their lives by the way they talk. Don't do it to your family and friends either because the information will not be appreciated. Instead, use this information to begin to make the connection for yourself, and practice it if you want your life to change, because even on the smallest level, if you change the way you talk, your experiences are going to change.

If you are a person with an illness who believes that it is fatal and that you are going to die and that life is no good because nothing ever works for you, then guess what?

You can choose to release your negative concept of life. Start affirming for yourself that you are a person who is lovable, and you are worth healing, and that you attract everything you need on the physical level to contribute to your healing. Know that you are willing to get well and that it is safe for you to get well.

Many people only feel safe when they are sick. They are usually the kind that have difficulty saying the word *no*. The only way they can say *no* is by saying, "I'm too sick to do it." It's a perfect excuse. I remember a woman at one of my workshops who had three cancer operations. She couldn't say *no* to anybody. Her father was a doctor, and she was Daddy's good little girl, so whatever daddy told her to do, she did. It was impossible for her to say *no*. No matter what you asked her, she had to say *yes*. It took four days to get her to literally shriek "No!" at the top of her lungs. I had her do it while shaking her fist. "No! No! No!" Once she got into it, she loved it.

I find that many women with breast cancer can't say *no*. They nourish everybody except themselves. One of the things I recommend to a woman with breast cancer is that she must learn to say, "No, I don't want to do it. No!" Two or three months of saying *no* to everything will begin to turn things around. She needs to nourish herself by saying, "This is what *I* want to do, not what *you* want me to do!"

When I used to work with clients privately, I would hear them argue on behalf of their limitations, and they would always want me to know why they were stuck because of one reason or another. If we believe we are stuck and accept that we are stuck, then we are stuck. We get "stuck" because our negative beliefs are being fulfilled. Instead, let's begin to focus on our strengths.

Many of you tell me that my tapes saved your lives. I want you to realize that no book or tape is going to save you. A little piece of tape in a plastic box is not saving your life. What you are doing with the information is what matters. I can give you plenty of ideas, yet what you do with them is going to count. I suggest that you listen to a particular tape over and over again for a month or more so that the ideas become a new habit pattern. I'm not your healer or savior. The only person who is going to make a change in your life is *you.*

Now, what are the messages you want to hear? I know I say this over and over again—*loving yourself is the most important thing you can do, because when you love yourself, you are not going to hurt yourself or anyone else.* It's the prescription for world peace. If I don't hurt me and I don't hurt you, how can we have war? The more of us who can get to that place, the better the planet will be. Let's begin to be conscious of what is going on by listening to the words we speak to ourselves and others. Then we can begin to make the changes that will help heal ourselves as well as the rest of the planet.

Chapter 4

Reprogramming Old Tapes

*Be willing to take the first step, no
matter how small it is. Concentrate on
the fact that you are willing to learn.
Absolute miracles will happen.*

Affirmations Do Work

Now that we understand a little bit more about how powerful our thoughts and words are, we have to retrain our thinking and speaking into positive patterns if we are going to get beneficial results. Are you willing to change your *self-talk* into positive affirmations? Remember, every time you think a thought, and every time you speak a word, you are saying an affirmation.

An affirmation is a beginning point. It opens the way to change. In essence you are saying to your subconscious mind, "I am taking responsibility. I am aware that there is something I can do to change." When I talk about *doing affirmations,* I mean to consciously choose sentences or words that will either help to eliminate something from your life or help to create something new in your life, and you do this in a positive way. If you say, "I don't want

33

to be sick anymore," the subconscious mind hears *sick more*. You have to tell it clearly what you do want. That is, say: *I am feeling wonderfully well. I radiate good health."*

The subconscious mind is very straightforward. It has no strategy or designs. What it hears is what it does. If you say, "I hate this car," it doesn't give you a wonderful new car, because it doesn't know what you want. Even if you get a new car, you will probably hate it soon, because that is what you have been saying about it. The subconscious only hears, *hate this car.* You need to clearly declare your desires in a positive way, as in: *'I have a beautiful new car that suits all my needs."*

If there is something in your life that you really dislike, I have found one of the quickest ways to release it is to bless it with love. *"I bless you with love and I release you and let you go."* This works for people, situations, objects, and living quarters. You could even try it on a habit you would like to be free of and see what happens. I had one man who said, "I bless you with love and release you from my life," to every cigarette he smoked. After a few days his desire for smoking was considerably less and in a few weeks the habit was gone.

You Deserve Good

Think for a moment. What is it you really want right now? What is it you want today in your life? Think about it, and then say, "I accept for myself _to start Traveling_ (whatever it is you want). This is where I find that most of us get stuck.

The bottom line is the belief that we don't deserve to have what we want. Our personal power lies in the way we perceive our deservability. Our not deserving comes from childhood messages. Again, we don't have to feel that we cannot change because of these messages. Often times, people will come up to me and say, "Louise, affirmations don't work." It really has nothing to do with the affirmations; it is the fact that we don't believe we deserve the good.

The way to find out if you believe that you deserve something is to say an affirmation and notice the thoughts that come up as you say it. Then write them down, because when you see them on paper, they will be very clear to you. The only thing that keeps you from deserving, or loving yourself, or whatever, is someone else's belief or opinion that you have accepted as truth.

When we don't believe that we deserve good, we will knock the pinnings out from under ourselves, which we can do in a variety of ways. We can create chaos, we can lose things, we can hurt ourselves, or have physical problems like falling, or have accidents. We have to start believing that we deserve all the good that life has to offer.

In order to reprogram the false or negative belief, what would be the first thought that you would need to begin to create this new "whatever" in your life? What would be the building block or the foundation that you would need to stand on? What would be the sort of thing that you would need to know for yourself? To believe? To accept?

✦ Some good thoughts to start with would be:

- *"I am worthwhile."*
- *"I am deserving."*
- *"I love myself."*
- *"I allow myself to be fulfilled."*

These concepts form the very basis of beliefs on which you can build. Do your affirmations on top of these building blocks to create what you want.

Whenever I speak somewhere, somebody will come up at the end of the lecture or will write me a letter and tell me that he or she has had a healing take place while he or she was in the room. Sometimes it's very minor, and sometimes it's quite dramatic. A woman came up to me recently and told me that she had a lump in her breast, and it literally disappeared during the lecture. She heard something, and she decided to let something go. This is a good example of how powerful we are. When we are not ready to let something go, when we really want to hold on to something because it is serving us in some way, it doesn't matter what we do, it probably won't work. However, when we are ready to let it go, as this woman was, it's amazing how the smallest circumstance can help us release it.

If you still have a habit that you haven't released, ask yourself how it serves you. What do you get out of it? If you can't get an answer, ask in a different way. "If I no longer had this habit, what would happen?" Very often the answer is, "My life would be better." It comes back to the fact that we believe we don't deserve a better life in some way.

Ordering from the Cosmic Kitchen

When you first say an affirmation, it may not seem true. But remember, affirmations are like planting seeds in the ground. When you put a seed in the ground, you don't get a full-grown plant the next day. We need to be patient during the growing season. As you continue to say the affirmation, either you will be ready to release whatever you don't want, and the affirmation will become true; or it will open a new avenue to you. Or, you may get a brilliant brainstorm, or a friend may call you and say, "Have you ever tried this?" You will be led to the next step that will help you.

Keep your affirmations in the present tense. You can sing them and make a jingle out of them so they repeat over and over in your head. Remember that you cannot affect a specific person's actions with your affirmations. To affirm that "John is now in love with me," is a form of manipulation, and it is trying to have control over another persons' life. It will usually have a boomerang effect on you. You will become very unhappy when you don't get what you want. You can say, "I am now loved by a wonderful man who is . . . . ," and list the qualities you want in the relationship. That way you allow the Power within you to bring to you the perfect person to fill that bill, who may possibly be John.

You don't know what another person's spiritual lesson is, and you don't have a right to interfere in their life process. You certainly wouldn't want someone else doing it to you. If someone is ill, bless them and send them love and peace, don't demand that they get well.

I like to think of doing affirmations as placing our order in the *cosmic kitchen*. If you go to a restaurant and the waiter or waitress comes and takes your order, you don't follow them into the kitchen to see if the chef got the order or how he is going to prepare the food. You sit and drink your water or coffee or tea or you talk to your friend, and maybe eat your roll. You assume that your food is being prepared and will be out when it is ready. It's the same when we begin to do affirmations.

When we put our order into the *cosmic kitchen,* the great chef, our Higher Power, is working on it. So you go on with your life and know it is being taken care of. It's on order. It's happening. Now if the food comes out and it isn't what you ordered, and if you have self-esteem, you will send it back. If not, you will eat it. You also have a right to do that with the *cosmic kitchen.* If you don't get exactly what you want, you can say, "No, that's not quite it; this is what I want." Perhaps, you weren't clear in your ordering.

The idea here, too, is to let go. At the end of my treatments and meditations, I use the words, *And so it is.* It is a way of saying, "Higher Power, it's in your hands now, I release it to you." Spiritual mind treatment, which is taught by the Science of Mind, is very effective. You can obtain more information about it through your local Religious Science Church or through books by Ernest Holmes.

Reprogramming the Subconscious Mind

The thoughts we think accumulate, and when we are unaware, the old thought resurfaces. When we are reprogramming our minds, it is normal and natural that we go a little forward, we come a little back, and we go a little forward again. It is part of practicing. I don't think there is any new skill that you can learn absolutely 100 percent in the first 20 minutes.

Do you remember when you first learned how to use a computer, how frustrating it was? It took practice. You had to learn how it worked, to learn its laws and systems. I called my first computer my Magic Lady, for when I mastered her rules she did indeed deliver what seemed like magic to me. Yet, while I was learning, the way she would teach me I was off track or going in the wrong direction, was to devour pages of work that I would then have to do over again. Out of all the mistakes, I learned how to flow with the system.

To flow with the system of Life, you want to become aware that your subconscious mind is like a computer—garbage in, garbage out. If you put negative thoughts in, then negative experiences come out. Yes, it takes time and practice to learn the new ways of thinking. Be patient with yourself. When you are learning something new, and the old pattern returns, are you going to say, "Oh, I didn't learn anything?" Or are you going to say, "Okay, that's all right, come on, let's do it again the new way."

Or, say you cleared an issue and think you'll never have to deal with it again. How do you know if you've really worked it through unless you test yourself? So, you bring up the old situation one more time and watch how you react. If you jump right back into the old way of reacting to it, then you know you haven't really learned that particular lesson, and you need to do more work on it. That's all it means. You have to realize it's a little test to see how far you've come. If you begin to repeat your affirmations, the new statements of truth about yourself, you give yourself an opportunity to react differently. Whether it's a health problem, a financial one, or a relationship difficulty, if you react in a new way to the situation, then you're on your way to having another issue handled, and you can move on to other areas.

Remember, too, that we work on layers at a time. You can reach a plateau and think, "I've done it!" And then some old issue resurfaces and you injure yourself, or get sick, and you don't get better for some time. Look to see what the underlying beliefs are. It may mean you have some more work to do because you are going to the next deeper layer.

Don't feel that you *are not good enough*, because something you have worked to clear comes up again. When I discovered that I was not a *bad person* because once again

I was facing an old issue, it became much easier for me to keep going. I learned to say to myself, "Louise, you are doing very well. Look how far you have come. You just need more practice. And I love you."

I believe each one of us decides to incarnate upon this planet at particular points in time and space. We have chosen to come here to learn a particular lesson that will advance us on our spiritual, evolutionary pathway.

One of the ways to allow the process of life to unfold for you in a positive, healthy way is to declare your own personal truths. Choose to move away from the limiting beliefs that have been denying you the benefits you so desire. Declare that your negative thought patterns will be erased from your mind. Let go of your fears and burdens. For a long time now, I have been believing the following ideas, and they have worked for me:

- *"Everything I need to know is revealed to me."*
- *"Everything I need comes to me in the perfect time-space sequence."*
- *"Life is a joy and filled with love."*
- *"I am loving and lovable and loved."*
- *"I am healthy and filled with energy."*
- *"I prosper wherever I turn."*
- *"I am willing to change and to grow,"* and
- *"All is well in my world."*

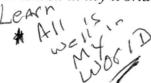

My God is an Awesome God!

I have learned that we don't always stay positive 100 percent of the time, and I include myself in this knowledge. As much as possible, I see life as a wonderful joyous experience. I believe that I am safe. I have made it a personal law for me.

I believe that everything I need to know is revealed to me, so I need to keep my eyes and ears open. When I had cancer, I remember thinking that a foot reflexologist would be very helpful for me. One evening I went to a lecture of some sort. Usually I sit in the front row because I like being close to the speaker; however that night I was compelled to sit in the back row. Right after I sat down, a foot reflexologist sat next to me. We began to talk and I learned that he even made house calls. I didn't have to look for him, he came to me.

I also believe that whatever I need comes to me in the perfect time-space sequence. When something goes wrong in my life, I immediately start to think, "All is well, it's okay, I know that this is all right. It's a lesson, an experience, and I'll pass through it. There is something here that is for my highest good. All is well. Just breathe. It's okay." I do the best I can to calm myself, so I can think rationally about whatever is going on, and, of course, I do work through everything. It may take a little time, but sometimes, things that seem to be great disasters really turn out to be quite good in the end, or at least, not the disasters that they seemed to be in the beginning. Every event is a learning experience.

I do a lot of positive *self-talk,* morning, noon and night. I come from a loving space of the heart, and I practice loving myself and others as much as I possibly can.

My love expands all the time. What I do today is much more than what I was doing six months or a year ago. I know a year from now my consciousness and my heart will have expanded, and I'll be doing more. I know that what I believe about myself becomes true for me, so I choose to believe wonderful things about myself. There was a time when I didn't, so I know I have grown, and I continue to work on myself.

I also believe in meditation. To me, meditation is when we sit down and turn off our inner dialogue long enough to hear our own wisdom. When I meditate, I usually close my eyes, take a deep breath and ask: *'What is it I need to know?'* I sit and listen. I might also ask, *'What is it I need to learn?'* or *'What is the lesson in this?'* Sometimes, we think we're supposed to *fix* everything in our lives, and maybe we're really only supposed to *learn* something from the situation.

When I first began to meditate, I had violent headaches the first three weeks. Meditation was so unfamiliar and against all my usual inner programming. Nevertheless, I hung in there, and the headaches eventually disappeared.

If you are constantly coming up with a tremendous amount of negativity when you meditate, it may mean that it *needs* to come up, and when you quiet yourself, it starts to flow to the surface. Simply see the negativity being released. Try not to fight it. Allow it to continue as long as it needs to.

If you fall asleep when you meditate, that's all right. Let the body do what it needs to do, it will balance out in time.

Reprogramming your negative beliefs is very powerful. A good way to do it is by making a tape *with your own voice* saying your affirmations. Play it as you go to sleep. It will have a great deal of value for you because you will be listening to your own voice. An even more powerful tape would be your mother's voice telling you how wonderful you are and how much she loves you. Once you have the tape, it's good to relax the body before you begin reprogramming. Some people like to start from the tips of their toes and move up to the top of their head, tensing and relaxing. However you do it, release the tension. Let the emotions go. Get to a state of openness and receptivity. The more relaxed you are, the easier it is to receive the new information. Remember, you are always in charge, and you are always safe.

It is wonderful to listen to tapes or read self-awareness books, and do your affirmations. But, what are you doing for the other 23 hours and 30 minutes of the day? You see, that is what really matters. If you sit down and meditate and then get up and rush to work and scream at someone, that counts, too. Meditation and affirmations are wonderful, yet the other times are just as important.

Treat Doubt as a Friendly Reminder

I am often asked questions about whether people are doing affirmations correctly or whether they are even working. I'd like you to think of *doubt* a little differently than you may have been. I believe that the subconscious mind resides in the solar plexus area of the body, where you carry those *gut feelings*. When something sudden happens don't you immediately get a strong feeling in your gut? It is where you take everything in and store it.

Ever since we were little children, every message we have received, everything we have done, all the experiences we have had, all that we have said, have all gone into the filing cabinet right there in the solar plexus area. I like to think that there are little messengers in there, and when we think thoughts or have experiences, the messages go in, and the messengers file them in the appropriate files. For many of us we have been building up files labeled: *I'm not good enough. I'll never make it. I don't do it right.* We have gotten absolutely buried under these files. Suddenly we do affirmations such as: *I'm wonderful and I love myself.* The messengers pick them up and say, "What's this??? Where does it go? We've never seen this one before!"

So the messengers call *Doubt.* "Doubt! Come over here and see what's going on." So *Doubt* picks up the message and asks the conscious mind, "What's this? You have always been saying these other things." On a conscious level we can react in two ways. We can say, "Oh you're right, I'm terrible. I'm no good. I'm sorry. That's not the right message," and go back to our old ways. Or we can say to *Doubt*, "That was the old message. I have no need for it now. This is the new message." Tell *Doubt* to start a new file because there will be lots of these loving messages coming through from now on. Learn to treat doubt as a friend, not the enemy, and thank it for questioning you.

It doesn't matter what you do in this world. It doesn't matter if you are a bank president or a dishwasher, a housewife or a sailor. You have wisdom inside of you that is connected to Universal Truth. When you are willing to look within and ask a simple question such as, "What is this experience trying to teach me?" and if you are willing to listen, then you will have the answer. Most of us are so busy running around creating the soap opera and drama we call our lives that we don't hear anything.

Don't give your power over to other people's pictures of right and wrong. They only have power over us when we give our power to them. Groups of people give their power over to others. It happens in a lot of cultures. Women in our culture give their power to men. They say things like, "My husband won't allow me to." Well that's certainly giving your power away. If you believe it, you box yourself into a place where you can't do anything unless you are given permission by another person. The more open-minded you are, the more you learn, and the more you can grow and change.

A woman once shared with me that when she got married she was very unassertive because that was the way she was brought up. It took years for her to realize that her conditioning kept her locked in a corner. She blamed everyone—her husband and her in-laws—for her problems. Eventually, she divorced her husband, however, she still blamed him for so many things that were not right in her life. It took her ten years to relearn her patterns and to take her power back. In hindsight, she realized that *she* was responsible for not speaking up and for not standing up for herself—not her husband or her in-laws. They were there to reflect back to her what she felt inside—a sense of powerlessness.

Don't give your power away based on what you read either. I remember years ago I read some articles in a well known magazine and I happened to know something about each subject described in the articles. In my opinion, the information was totally erroneous. The magazine lost all credibility for me, and I didn't read it again for many years. You are the authority in your life, so don't think that because something is in print that it's always the truth.

Inspirational speaker Terry Cole-Whittaker wrote a wonderful book called *What You Think Of Me Is None Of My Business*. It's true. What you think of me *is* none of my business—it's *your* business. In the end, what you think of me is going out from you in vibrations and will come back.

When we have illumination, when we become conscious of what we are doing, we can begin to change our lives. Life is really here for *you*. You need only ask. Tell life what you want, and then allow the good to happen.

PART TWO

Dissolving the Barriers

We want to know what is going on inside us, so we can know what to let go. Instead of hiding our pain, we can release it totally.

Chapter 5

Understanding the Blocks That Bind You

Chronic patterns of self-hate, guilt, and self-criticism raise the body's stress levels and weaken the immune system.

Now that we understand a little more about the power that we have within us, let's take a look at what keeps us from using it. I think that almost all of us have barriers of some kind or another. Even when we do a lot of work on ourselves, and clear out the blocks, new layers of old barriers still keep coming up.

Many of us feel so flawed that we believe that we are not good enough and never will be. And, if we find something wrong with us, then we are going to find something wrong with other people as well. If we are still continuing to say, "I can't do this because my mother said . . . , or my father said . . . ," then we have not yet grown up.

So now you want to let your barriers go, and perhaps learn something different that you didn't know before now. Perhaps one sentence here will trigger a new thought. Can you imagine how wonderful it would be if every day you learned a new idea that would help you let go of the past and create harmony in your life? When you become aware and understand the individual process of life,

51

you will know what direction to take. If you put your energies into learning about yourself, you will eventually see those problems and issues that you need to dissolve.

We all have challenges in life. Everybody does. Nobody goes through life without them; otherwise, what would be the purpose of coming to this particular school called Earth? For some, there are health challenges, and for other people there are relationship challenges, or career or financial challenges. Some have a little or a lot of everything.

I think one of our biggest problems is that most of us haven't the faintest idea of what it is we want to let go. We know what is not working and we know what we want in our life, yet we don't know what's holding us back. So let's take this time to look at the blocks that bind us.

If you think for a moment about your own patterns and problems and the things that hold you back, which categories do they fall into—*criticism, fear, guilt, or resentment*? I call these categories, *The Big Four*. Which is your favorite one? Mine was a combination of criticism and resentment. Maybe you are like me and have two or three. Is it fear that always comes up, or guilt? Are you very, very critical or resentful? Let me point out that resentment is anger that is stuffed down. So if you believe you are not allowed to express your anger, then you have stored a lot of resentment.

We cannot deny our feelings. We cannot conveniently ignore them. When I had my cancer diagnosis, I had to look very clearly at myself. I had to acknowledge some nonsense that I didn't want to admit about myself. For instance, I was a very resentful person, and I carried a lot of bitterness from the past. I said, "Louise, you have no time to indulge in that anymore. You really must change." Or as Peter Mc Williams says, "You can no longer afford the luxury of a negative thought." ·

Your experiences always reflect your inner beliefs. You can literally look at your experiences and determine what your beliefs are. Maybe it's disturbing to consider, but if you look at the people in your life, they are all mirroring some belief you have about yourself. If you are always being criticized at work, it is probably because you are critical and have become the parent who once criticized the child. Everything in our lives is a mirror of who we are. *pos/* When something is happening out there that is not comfortable, we have an opportunity to look inside and say, "How am I contributing to this experience? What is it within me that believes I deserve this?"

We all have family patterns, and it is very easy for us to blame our parents, or our childhood, or our environment, but that keeps us stuck. We don't become free. We remain victims, and we perpetuate the same problems over and over again.

So it really doesn't matter what anybody else did to you or what they taught you in the past. Today is a new day. You are now in charge. Now is the moment in which you are creating the future in your life and your world. It really doesn't matter what I say either, because only *you* can do the work. Only you can change the way you think and feel and act. I'm just saying that you *can*. You definitely can because you have a Higher Power within you that can help break you free from these patterns if you allow It.

You can remind yourself that when you were a little baby, you loved yourself for who you were. There is not one little baby who criticizes its body and thinks, "Oh, my hips are too big." Babies are thrilled and delighted just because they have bodies. They express their feelings. When a baby is happy, you know it, and when a baby is angry, the whole neighborhood knows it. They are never afraid to let people know how they feel. They live in the moment. You were like that once. As you grew up, you listened to people around you, and learned about fear and guilt and criticism from them.

If you grew up in a family where criticism was the norm, then you are going to be critical as an adult. If you grew up in a family where you were not allowed to express anger, then you are probably terrified of anger and confrontation, and you swallow it and let it reside in your body.

If you were raised in a family where everybody was manipulated by guilt, then you are probably going to be the same way as an adult. You are probably a person who runs around saying "I'm sorry" all the time, and can never ask for anything outright. You feel you have to be manipulative in some way in order to get what you want.

As we grow up, we begin to pick up these false ideas and lose touch with our inner wisdom. So we really need to release these ideas and return to the purity of spirit where we truly love ourselves. We need to re-establish the wonderful innocence of life and the moment-by-moment joy of existence, the same joy that a baby feels in its blissful state of wonder.

Think of what you want to become true for yourself. State them in positive, not negative affirmations. Now, go to the mirror and repeat your affirmations. See what obstacles are in your way. When you begin to state an affirmation like, *"I love and approve of myself,"* really pay attention to what negative messages come up because as you recognize them they become the treasures that will unlock the door to your freedom. Usually, the messages are one of the four I mentioned earlier—criticism, fear, guilt, or resentment. And, most likely you learned these messages from people "back there."

Some of you have chosen some difficult tasks to handle in this lifetime, and it is my belief that we really come here to love ourselves in spite of what *they* say or do. We can always go beyond our parents' or our friends' limitations. If you were a good little girl or boy, you learned your parents' limited way of looking at life. You see, you are not bad; you are ideal children. You learned exactly what your parents taught you. Now that you are grown up, you're doing the same thing. How many of you hear yourself saying what your parents used to say? Congratulations! They were very good teachers and you were very good students, but now it is time for you to begin to think for yourself.

A lot of us may face resistance when we look in the mirror and repeat our affirmations. However, resistance is the first step to change. Most of us want our lives to change, but when we are told that we have to do something different, we say, "Who me? I don't want to do that."

Others may experience feelings of despair. Often, if you look at the mirror and say, "I love you," the little child inside says, "Where have you been all this time? I've been waiting for you to notice me." Waves of sadness come up because you have been rejecting the little child for a long, long time.

When I did this exercise in one of my workshops, a woman said she was very, very scared. I asked her what frightened her, and she shared the fact that she was an incest survivor. Many of us have had this experience called incest and we are learning to come through it. It's interesting that it occurs so often on our planet. We read so much about incest these days, yet I don't think it is happening any more now than it ever did. We have advanced to a state where we now feel that children have rights and we are allowing ourselves to see this ugly sore in society. In order to release the problem, we have to first recognize it and then we can work through it.

Therapy is so important for incest survivors. We need a safe space where we can work through these feelings. When we have let the anger and rage and shame out then we move to the space where we can love ourselves. No matter what we are working on we want to remember that the feelings that come up are *just* feelings. We are not in the experience anymore. We need to work on making the inner child feel safe. We have to thank ourselves for having had the courage to survive this experience. Sometimes when we are dealing with an issue such as incest, it's difficult to accept that the other person was doing the best he or she could at the time with the understanding and awareness and knowledge that they had. Acts of violence always come from people who were violated themselves. We all need healing. When we learn to love and cherish who we are, we will no longer harm anyone.

Stop All Criticism

When we are dealing with criticism, we are usually criticizing ourselves all the time for the same things over and over. When are we going to wake up and learn that criticism doesn't work? Let's try another tactic. Let's approve of ourselves as we are right now. Critical people often attract a lot of criticism because it is their pattern to criticize. What we give out, we get back. They may also need to be perfect at all times. Who's perfect? Have you ever met a perfect person? I haven't. If we complain about another person, we are really complaining about some aspect of ourselves.

Everyone is a reflection of us, and what we see in another person, we see in ourselves. Many times we don't want to accept parts of who we are. We abuse ourselves with alcohol or drugs or cigarettes or overeating or whatever. These are ways of beating up on ourselves for not being perfect—but, being perfect for who? Whose early demands and expectations are we still trying to meet? Be willing to let that go. Just *be.* You will find that you are wonderful just as you are this very moment.

If you have always been a critical person who sees life through very negative eyes, it is going to take time for you to turn yourself around to be more loving and accepting. You will learn to be patient with yourself as you practice letting go of the criticism which is only a habit, not the reality of your being.

Can you imagine how wonderful it would be if we could live our lives without ever being criticized by anyone? We would feel totally at ease, totally comfortable. Every morning would be a wonderful new day because everyone would love you and accept you and nobody would criticize you or put you down. You can give this happiness to yourself by becoming more accepting of the things that make you unique and special.

The experience of living with yourself can be the most wonderful experience imaginable. You can wake up in the morning and feel the joy of spending another day with you.

When you love who you are, you automatically bring out the best in you. I'm not saying you will be a better person because that implies that you are not good enough now. However, you will find more positive ways to fulfill your needs, and to express more of who you really are.

Guilt Makes Us Feel Inferior

Many times people give you negative messages because it is the easiest way to manipulate you. If someone is trying to make you feel guilty, ask yourself, "What do they want? Why are they doing this?" Ask these questions instead of inwardly agreeing, "Yes, I'm guilty, I must do what they say."

Many parents manipulate their children with guilt because they were raised the same way. They tell lies to their children to make them feel *less than*. Some people are still manipulated by their relatives and friends when they grow up because, first of all, they don't respect themselves, otherwise they wouldn't let it happen. Secondly, they are manipulative themselves.

Many of you live under a cloud of guilt. You always feel *wrong*, or that you are not doing the right thing, or apologizing to someone for something. You will not forgive yourself for something you did in the past. You berate yourself for a lot that goes on in your life. Let the cloud dissipate. You don't need to live that way any longer.

Those of you who feel guilty can now learn to say *no* and call people on their nonsense. I'm not saying to be angry with them, but you don't have to play their game anymore. If saying "no" is new to you, say it very simply: "No. No, I cannot do that." Don't give excuses or the manipulator will have ammunition to talk you out of your decision. When people see that manipulating you doesn't work, they will stop. People will only control you as long as you allow them to. You may feel guilty the first time you say no; however, it gets easier the next few times.

A woman at one of my lectures had a baby who was born with congenital heart dis-ease. She felt guilty because she believed that it was her fault—she did something to the baby. Unfortunately, guilt does not solve anything. In her case, no one did anything wrong. I told her that I thought it could have been a soul choice for the baby, and a lesson for both the mother and baby. My answer was for her to love the baby and love herself and stop feeling that she did something wrong. That sort of guilt would not heal anyone.

If you do something that you are sorry about, stop doing it. If you did something in the past that you still feel guilty about, forgive yourself. If you can make amends, do it, and don't repeat the action again. Every time guilt comes up in your life, ask yourself, "What do I still believe about myself?" "Who am I trying to please?" Notice the childhood beliefs that come up.

When someone comes to me who has been involved in a car accident, there is usually guilt on a deep-seated level and a need for punishment. There can also be a lot of repressed hostility because we feel we don't have the right to speak up for ourselves. Guilt seeks punishment, so we can literally become our own judge, jury, and executioner—condemning ourselves to a self-imposed prison. We punish ourselves, and there is no one around to come to our defense. It's time to forgive ourselves and set ourselves free.

One elderly lady at one of my seminars felt enormous guilt about her middle-aged son. He was an only child who grew up to be a very withdrawn person. She felt guilty because she was very strict with him while he was growing up. I explained that she had done the best she knew how to do at the time. I believe he chose her as a mother before he incarnated into this lifetime, so on a spiritual level, he knew what he was doing. I told her that she was wasting all her energy feeling guilty about something that she couldn't change. She sighed, "It's such a shame that he's this way, and I'm sorry I did a bad job."

You see, that's wasted energy because it doesn't help her son now, and it certainly doesn't help her. Guilt becomes a very heavy burden and makes people feel inferior.

Instead, I told her that every time the feeling came up, she could say something like, "No, I don't want to feel that anymore. I'm willing to learn to love myself. I accept my son exactly as he is." If she continued to do this, the pattern would start to shift.

Even if we don't know how to love ourselves, the fact that we are *willing* to love ourselves will create the difference. It's just not worth it to hold on to these patterns. The lesson is always *love yourself*. Her lesson was not to heal her son, but to love herself. He came into this life to love himself. She can't do it for him, and he can't do it for her.

Organized religions are often really good at making people feel guilty. Many of them do some heavy numbers to keep people in line, especially when they are young. However, we aren't little children anymore, and we don't have to be kept in line. We are adults who can decide what we want to believe. The child in us feels the guilt, but there is also the adult in us who can teach the child otherwise.

When you hold your emotions down, or hold things in, you create havoc within you. Love yourself enough to allow yourself to feel your emotions. Allow your feelings to come to the surface. You may find yourself crying for days or getting angry a lot. You may have to process quite a bit of old stuff. I suggest you do affirmations that make going through the process easier, smoother, and more comfortable:

- *"I now release with ease all old negative beliefs."*
- *"It's comfortable for me to change."*
- *"My pathway is now smooth."*
- *"I am free of the past."*

Don't also add judgment to your feelings. That only pushes the feelings down even more. If you are going through incredible dilemmas or crises, affirm that you are safe and that you are willing to feel. Affirming these positive feelings will bring about beneficial changes.

Chapter 6

Letting Your Feelings Out

*A tragedy can turn out to be our
greatest good if we approach it in
ways from which we can grow.*

Releasing Anger in Positive Ways

Everyone deals with anger at one time or another in their
lives. Anger is an honest emotion. When it is not expressed
or processed outwardly, it will be processed inwardly, in
the body, and usually develops into a dis-ease or dysfunction of some sort.

Like criticism, we usually get angry about the same
things over and over again. When we are angry, and we
feel we don't have a right to express it, we swallow it
down, which causes resentment, bitterness, or depression.
So, its good to *handle* our anger when it comes up.

There are several ways to deal with anger in positive
ways. One of the best ways is to talk openly to the person with whom you are angry and to release the pent-up
emotions. You can say, "I am angry with you because
_____." When we feel like screaming at some-
one, then the anger has been building up for a long time.

Often, it is because we feel we cannot speak to the other person. So, the second best way to let the anger out is to talk to the person in the mirror.

Find yourself a place where you will feel safe and will not be disturbed. Look into your own eyes in the mirror. If you find that you cannot, then concentrate on your mouth or nose. See yourself and/or the person who you believe has done something wrong to you. Remember the moment when you became angry and let yourself feel the anger come through you. Begin to tell this person exactly what you are so angry about. Show all the anger you feel. You could say something like:

- *"I am angry at you because* _____*."*
- *"I am hurt because you did* _____*."*
- *"I am so afraid because you* _____*."*

Get all your feelings out. If you feel like expressing yourself physically, then get some pillows and start hitting them. Don't be afraid to let your anger take its natural course. You have already kept your feelings bottled up too long. There is no need to feel any guilt or shame. Remember, our feelings are thoughts in action. They serve a purpose, and when you let them loose from your mind and body, you allow space inside for other, more positive, experiences.

When you have finished expressing your anger to the person or persons, do your best to forgive them. Forgiveness is an act of freedom for yourself because you are the one who will benefit from it. If you can't forgive someone, then the exercise is just a negative affirmation and is not healing for you. There is a difference between *releasing* and just *rehashing* old angers. You may want to say something like:

> *"Okay, that situation is over. That is in the past now. I don't approve of your action, and yet I understand that you were doing the best you could with the knowledge and understanding you had at the time. I am done with this. I release you and let you go. You are free and I am free."*

You may want to do this exercise several times before you truly feel that you have gotten rid of all of your anger. You may also want to work on one anger issue or several. Do what feels right for you.

There are other methods we can use to release the anger. We can scream into a pillow, we can kick pillows, we can beat the bed or a punching bag. We can write a *hate letter* and then burn it. We can scream in our cars with the windows rolled up. We can play tennis or go to the golf range and just hit balls one after the other. We can exercise, swim, or run around the block several times. We can write or draw our feelings using our nondominant hand— the creative process is a natural release for emotions.

One man at my seminar said he used an egg timer as he began screaming into a pillow. He gave himself ten minutes to let out all his frustrations and anger about his father. After five minutes, he was exhausted, and every thirty seconds, he would look at the egg timer and realize he still had a few more minutes to go.

I used to beat the bed and make a lot of noise. I can't do that now because my dogs get frightened and think I am angry at them. Now I find it very effective to scream in the car, or dig a hole in the garden.

As you can see, you can become quite creative when releasing your feelings. I recommend that you do something physically to release charged-up emotions—in a safe way. Don't be reckless or dangerous to yourself or others. Remember, also, to communicate with your Higher Power. Go within and know that there is an answer to your anger and that you will find it. It is very healing to meditate and visualize your rage flowing freely out of your body. Send love to the other person, and see your love dissolve whatever disharmony there is between you. Be willing to become harmonious. Perhaps the anger you feel is reminding you that you aren't communicating well with others. By recognizing it, you can correct it.

It's amazing how many people tell me how much happier they have become once they release anger towards another person. It is as though a huge burden has been dropped. One of my students had a difficult time letting her anger out. Intellectually, she understood her feelings, yet she couldn't express them outwardly. Once she allowed herself this expression, she kicked and screamed and called her mother and alcoholic daughter all sorts of names. She felt a tremendous weight lift from her. When her daughter visited her afterwards, she couldn't stop hugging her. She allowed room for love to come inside where all the repressed anger had been.

Maybe you have been a person who's been angry for a major part of your life. You have, what I call, *habitual anger*. Something happens and you get angry. Something else happens and you get angry again. Once more it happens, and you keep getting angry, but you never go beyond getting angry. Habitual anger is childish—you always want your own way. It would be helpful to ask yourself:

- *"Why am I choosing to be angry all the time?"*
- *"What am I doing to create situation after situation that angers me?"*
- *"Is this the only way I can react to life?"*
- *"Is this what I want?"*
- *"Who am I still punishing? Or loving?"*
- *"Why do I want to be in this state?"*
- *"What am I believing that causes all these frustrations?"*
- *"What am I giving out that attracts in others the need to irritate me?"*

In other words, why do you believe that to get your way, you need to get angry? I'm not saying that there are no injustices, and there aren't times when you have a right to feel angry. However, habitual anger is not good for your body because it lodges in there.

Notice what you focus on most of the time. Sit in front of a mirror for ten minutes and look at yourself. Ask: *'Who are you? What is it that you want? What makes you happy? What can I do to make you happy?'* Now is the time to do something else. Create a new space inside yourself for loving, optimistic, and cheerful patterns.

People often get angry while they are driving their cars. People often express their frustrations about the other lousy drivers on the road. Long ago, I got over the fact that I was going to be upset because of someone else's inability to follow the rules of the road. So the way I handle driving my car is: first, I put love into the car when I get in. Next, I know and affirm that I'm always surrounded by wonderful, competent, happy drivers. Everyone around me is a good driver. Because of my beliefs and affirmations whenever I'm on the road, I have very few poor drivers around me. They're off bothering the person who's shaking his fist and screaming.

Your car is an extension of you, just like everything and everyone are extensions of you, so put some love into your car, and then send love out to everyone around you on the streets and the highways. I believe, that the parts of your car are similar to the parts of your body.

For instance, one of my workers felt that she had "no vision," she could not see where her life was going or where she wanted it to go. One morning she woke up and found her windshield smashed. Another person, an acquaintance of mine, felt that he was "stuck" in his life. He was not moving forward or moving backwards but was not moving at all. His tire became flat and he couldn't move anywhere. I know it may sound silly at first, but it's fascinating to me that the terminology that these two people used to describe their current mental state also related to their car. "Having no vision" means that you can't see in front of you. The windshield is a perfect metaphor, likewise "being stuck" is a perfect example of a flat tire. The next time something happens to your car, make a note as to what you feel the broken part represents and see if you can connect it to how you are feeling at that particular moment. You may be surprised at the results. One day I will write a little book and call it *Heal Your Automobile*.

There was a time when people did not understand the body/mind connection. Now it is time for us to expand our thinking even more and to understand the machinery/mind connection. Every situation in your life is a learning experience and can be handled so that it works for you.

There is nothing new or unique about anger. No one escapes the experience. The key is in recognizing it for what it is and taking that energy in a healthier direction. If you get sick, don't get angry over it. Instead of putting anger into your body, fill it with love and forgive yourself. Those of you who are caregivers for sick people can remember to take care of yourselves, too. If you don't, you won't be any good to yourself or your friends and family. You will burn out. Do something to let your feelings out as well. Once you learn to deal with anger in a positive way that readily benefits you, you will find many wonderful changes occurring in the quality of your life.

Resentment Causes a Variety of Ills

Resentment is anger that has been buried for a long time. The main problem with resentment is that it lodges in the body, usually in the same place, and in time, it seethes and eats away at the body and often turns into tumors and cancers. Therefore, repressing anger and letting it settle in our bodies is not conducive to good health. Again, it's time to let these feelings out.

Many of us were raised in families where we weren't allowed to be angry. Women, in particular, were taught that to be angry was something *bad*. Anger was not acceptable, except for one person, usually a parent. So we learned to swallow our anger rather than express it. Again, we can now realize that we are the ones who are holding on to it. Nobody else is involved at all.

An oyster takes a grain of sand, and it builds layer after layer after layer of calcite over it until it becomes a beautiful pearl. Similarly, we take our emotional hurts and nurse them over and over again, by what I call, running the old movie over and over in our minds. If we want to be free from our hurts, if we want to get out of them, then it's time to go beyond them.

One of the reasons women create cysts and tumors in the uterus is through, what I call, the *he done me wrong syndrome*. The genitals represent either the most masculine part of the body, the masculine principle, or the most feminine part of the body, the feminine principle. When people have emotional episodes, usually in relationships, they take it to one of these areas. With women, they may take it to their female organs, their most feminine part, and nurse the hurt until it becomes a cyst or tumor.

Since resentment is buried deeply inside us, we may have to do a lot of work to dissolve it. I received a letter from a woman who was working on her third cancer tumor. She still had not dissolved the resentment pattern and kept creating new tumors in her body. I could tell she felt very self-righteous about her bitterness. It was easier for her to let the doctor remove the latest tumor than to work on forgiveness. It would have been good if she was able to do both. Doctors are good at removing growths, only we can keep them from re-appearing.

Sometimes we would rather die than change our patterns. And we do. I have noticed many people would rather die than change their eating habits. And they do. This is very disturbing when it happens to someone we love and we are aware of alternative choices they could make.

No matter what choices we make, they are always right for us and there is no blame, even if we leave the planet. We will all leave the planet in time and we will all find a way to do it at the right time for us.

Again, we don't have to blame ourselves for failing or doing it wrong. We don't have to feel guilty. There is no blame. No one has done it *wrong*. A person does the best he or she knows how to with the understanding and awareness that is available. Remember, we all have the Power within us, and we have all come here to learn certain lessons. Our Higher Selves know our destiny in this lifetime and what we learn in order to move forward in our evolutionary process. There is never any wrong way, there just *is*. We are all on an endless journey through eternity, and we have lifetime after lifetime. What we don't work out in this life, I believe we will work out in another.

I don't Believe This

Suppressed Feelings Lead to Depression

Depression is anger turned inward. It is also anger that you feel you do not have a right to have. For instance you may not feel it's okay to be angry at your parent or spouse or employer or best friend. Yet you are angry. And you feel stuck. That anger becomes depression. Far too many people today suffer from depression, even chronic depression. By the time we feel that depressed, it is very difficult to get out of it. It feels so hopeless that it becomes an effort to do anything.

I don't care how spiritual you are, you have got to wash your dishes every now and then. You can't let the sink pile up with dirty dishes and say, "Oh, I'm metaphysical." The same with your feelings, if you want to have a mind that flows freely then clean up your inner mental *dirty dishes*.

One of the best ways is to give yourself permission to express some of your anger so that you don't have to stay so depressed. There are now therapists that specialize in anger releasing. Having a session or two with one of them could be most helpful.

It's my personal opinion that we all need to beat the bed once a week whether we feel we're angry or not. There are some therapies that encourage you to get into your anger; however, I think they often keep you immersed in the anger process too long. Anger, like any emotion that surfaces, lasts only a few minutes. Babies move in and out of their emotions very quickly. It is our reaction to the emotion that causes us to hold and repress it.

Author Elisabeth Kübler-Ross uses a wonderful exercise in her seminars, she calls *externalization*. She has you take a piece of rubber hose and some old phone books, and you beat them over and over again, letting all sorts of emotions emerge.

When you are releasing anger, it's okay to be embarrassed about it, especially if it was against your family rules to get angry. It will be embarrassing the first time you do it, but when you get into it, it can be such fun and very powerful. God is not going to hate you for being angry. Once you have released some of this old anger, you will be able to see your situation in a new light and find new solutions.

Another one of the suggestions I would make for a person who is depressed is to work with a good nutritionist and really get your diet cleaned up. Its amazing how that can help the mind. People who are depressed often eat very poorly which adds to the problem. We all want to make the best choices so that the food we are taking in is good for our body. Also, many times we find there is a chemical imbalance in the body that is further aggravated by the intake of medication of some sort.

Rebirthing is another wonderful process for releasing your feelings because it goes beyond the intellect. If you have never had a rebirthing session, I recommend that you try it. It has been very helpful for many people. It's a breathing modality that helps you connect with old issues so that you can release them in a positive way. Some rebirthers have you repeat your affirmations as you are going through the process.

Then there is body work, such as Rolfing, a process of deep connective-tissue manipulation, developed by Ida Rolf. Or Heller work, or Trager work. They are all excellent ways to release restrictive patterns in the body. Different processes work differently for each person. One process may be good for one, yet not for another. We can only find what is best for ourselves by trying different avenues.

Self Help sections in book stores are excellent places to read about different alternatives. Health Food stores often have bulletin boards that list meetings and classes. When the student is ready, the teacher appears.

Fear Is Not Having Trust

Fear is rampant on the planet. You can see and hear about it in the news every day in the form of wars, murders, greed, and more. Fear is a lack of trust in ourselves. Because of that we don't trust Life. We don't trust that we are being taken care of on a higher level, so we feel we must control everything from the physical level. Obviously, we are going to feel fear because we can't control everything in our lives.

Trust is what we learn when we want to overcome our fears. It's called taking the *leap-of-faith*. Trust in the Power within that is connected to Universal Intelligence. Trust in that which is invisible, instead of trusting only in the physical, material world. I'm not saying that we do nothing, yet if we have trust, we can go through life much easier. If you recall what I said earlier, I believe that everything I need to know is revealed to me. I trust that I am being taken care of, even though I am not physically in control of everything that is happening around me.

When a fearful thought comes up, it really is trying to protect you. I suggest that you say to the fear, "I know you want to protect me. I appreciate that you want to help me. And I thank you." Acknowledge the fearful thought; it's there to take care of you. When you become physically frightened, your adrenalin pumps through your body to protect you from danger. It's the same with the fear you manufacture in your mind.

Observe your fears and recognize that you are not them. Think of fear the way you view images on a movie screen. What you see on the screen is really not there. The moving pictures are just frames of celluloid, and they change and disappear very rapidly. Our fears will come and go as rapidly as those pictures, unless we insist on holding on to them.

Fear is a limitation of our minds. People have so much fear about getting sick or about becoming homeless or whatever. Anger is fear that becomes a defense mechanism. It protects you and yet it would be much more powerful for you to do affirmations so you can stop recreating fearful situations in your minds, and love yourself through the fear. Again, nothing comes from outside of us. We are at the center of everything that happens in our lives. Everything is inside—every experience, every relationship, is the mirror of a mental pattern that we have inside us.

Fear is the opposite of love. The more we are willing to love and trust who we are, the more we attract these qualities to ourselves. When we are on a streak of really being frightened or upset or worried or not liking ourselves, isn't it amazing how everything goes wrong in our lives? One thing after another. It seems it will never stop.

Well, it is the same when we really love ourselves. Everything starts to go on a winning streak and we get the "green lights" and the "parking places." All of the things that make life so wonderful—the big and the little. We get up in the morning, and the day flows beautifully.

Love yourself so that you can take care of yourself. Do everything you can to strengthen your heart, your body, and your mind. Turn to the Power within you. Find a good spiritual connection, and really work on maintaining it.

If you are feeling threatened or fearful, consciously breathe. We often hold our breath when we are frightened. So take a few deep breaths. Breathing opens the space inside you that is your power. It straightens your spine. It opens your chest and gives your heart room to expand. By breathing you begin to drop the barriers and open up. You expand rather than contract. Your love flows. Say: "*I am one with the Power that created me. I am safe. All is well in my world.*"

Cleaning Up Our Addictions

One of the primary ways we mask our fears is through addictions. Addictions suppress the emotions, so that we don't feel. However, there are many kinds of addictions besides the chemical ones. There are also, what I call, pattern addictions—patterns we adopt to keep us from being present in our lives. If we don't want to deal with what's in front of us, or if we don't want to be where we are, we have a pattern that keeps us out of touch with our lives. For some people, it is a food addiction or a chemical addiction. There may be a genetic disposition for alcoholism, however, the choice to stay sick is always an individual one. So often, when we talk about something being hereditary, it is really the little child's acceptance of the parents' ways of handling fear.

For others, there are emotional addictions. You can be addicted to finding fault in people. No matter what happens, you will always find someone to blame. "It's their fault, they did it to me."

Maybe you are addicted to running up bills. There are many of you addicted to being in debt; you do everything to keep yourselves over your heads in debt. It doesn't seem to have anything to do with the amount of money you have.

You can be addicted to rejection. Everywhere you go, you attract others who reject you. You will find them. However, the rejection on the outside is a reflection of your own rejection. If you don't reject yourself, nobody else will either, or if they do, it certainly won't matter to you. Ask yourself, "What am I not accepting about myself?"

There are plenty of people addicted to illness. They are always catching something or worrying about getting sick. They seem to belong to the "Illness of the Month Club."

If you're going to be addicted to anything, why not be addicted to loving yourself? You can be addicted to do-

ing positive affirmations or doing something that is supportive of you.

Compulsive Overeating

I receive a lot of letters from people with weight problems. They go on diets that last two or three weeks, then
they stop. They feel guilty about falling off their diets, and
instead of recognizing that they did what they could at the
time, they get angry at themselves and feel guilty. Then
to punish themselves, because guilt always seeks punishment, they go out and eat foods that are not good for
their bodies. If they could acknowledge that for the two
weeks they followed a particular regime they were doing
something wonderful for their bodies and stop laying guilt
trips on themselves, they would begin to break the pattern. They could also begin to say: *"I used to have a
problem with weight, now I allow myself to be the perfect weight for me,"* and the pattern would start to shift
inside. Yet we don't want to concentrate on the food issue too much for that is *not* where the problem lies.

Overeating has always meant a need for protection.
When you feel insecure or frightened, you pad yourself
with a layer of safety. Weight has nothing to do with
food. Most of you spend a lifetime being angry at yourselves for being fat. What a waste of energy. Instead, realize there is something going on in your life that is making
you feel unsafe and insecure. It could be your work, your
spouse, your sexuality, or your life in general. If you are
overweight, put the food/weight issue aside and work

on the pattern that says, "I need protection because I'm insecure."

It's amazing how our cells respond to our mental patterns. When the need for protection is gone, or when we start feeling secure, the fat will melt off. I have noticed in my own life that when I am not feeling safe, I will gain some weight. When my life is going so fast, and I'm doing so much, and I'm spreading myself all over the place, I feel a need for protection, a need for security. So I say, "Okay, Louise, it's time to work on safety. I want you to really know that you are safe, and it's okay, and you can do all this stuff, and you can be at all these places, and you can have all that is happening right now, and you are safe, and I love you."

Weight is only the outer effect of a fear that is inside you. When you look in the mirror and see the fat person staring back, remember that you are looking at the result of your old thinking. When you start to change your thinking, you are planting a seed for what will become true for you. What you choose to think today will create your new figure tomorrow. One of the best books on releasing excess weight is *The Only Diet There Is* by Sondra Ray. It's all about dieting from negative thinking. She shows you step by step how to do it.

Self Help Groups

Self Help Groups have become the new social form. I see this as a very positive move. These programs do tremendous good. People with similar problems getting together not to whine and complain, but to find ways to work through these issues and improve the quality of their lives. There is now a group for almost every problem you can think of. Many of them are listed in the phone book under *Community Services* in the front of your Yellow Pages or see Appendix B in the back of this book (page 233). I know you can find one that is right for you. Many churches now hold group meetings.

You could even go to the local health food store, one of my favorites, and see what is listed on their bulletin board. If you are serious about changing your life, you will find the way.

The 12-Step Programs are everywhere. 12-Step Programs have been around for some time and they have developed a format that really works and bring about wonderful results. Their Al-Anon program for people who live with, or were raised by, addicted people is one of the best groups for all sorts of people.

Feelings Are Our Inner Gauge

When growing up in a troubled or dysfunctional family, we learn to avoid conflict whenever possible, and this results in the denial of our feelings. We often do not trust others to meet our needs so we don't even ask for help. We are convinced that we must be strong enough to handle things ourselves. The only problem is that we fail to be in touch with our own feelings. Feelings are our most helpful link to our relationship with ourselves, others and the world around us, and they are an indication of what's

working or not working in our lives. Shutting them off
only leads to more complex problems and physical illnesses. What you can feel, you can heal. If you don't allow yourself to feel what is going on inside of you, you
won't know where to begin the healing process.

On the other hand, many of us seem to go through life
always feeling guilty or jealous or fearful or sad. We develop habit patterns that keep perpetuating the same experiences that we say we don't want to have. If you keep
feeling angry, or sad, or fearful, or jealous and don't get
in touch with the underlying cause, you will continue to
create more anger, sad, fear, et cetera. When we stop feeling like victims, we are able to take our power back. We
must be willing to learn the lesson so the problem can
disappear.

When we trust the process of life and our spiritual connection with the Universe, we can dissolve our angers and
fears as soon as they appear. We *can* trust in life and
know that everything is happening in divine right order
and the perfect time-space sequence.

Chapter 7

Moving Beyond the Pain

*We are far more than our bodies and
personalities. The inner spirit is always
beautiful and lovable, no matter how
our outer appearances may change.*

The Pain of Death

It's wonderful to be positive. It's also wonderful to acknowledge what you are feeling. Nature has given you
feelings to get you through certain experiences and to
deny them causes more pain. Remember, death is not a
failure. Everyone dies, it's part of the process of life.

When someone you love dies, the mourning process
takes at least one year. So give yourself that space. It's difficult to have to go through all the holidays and seasons—
Valentine's Day, your birthday, your anniversary, Christ-
mas, et cetera, so be very gentle with yourself and let
yourself grieve. There are no rules, so don't make any for
yourself.

It's also okay to get angry and have hysterics when
someone dies. You can't pretend it doesn't hurt. You
want to give your feelings an outlet. Let yourself cry.
Look in the mirror and scream, "It isn't fair," or whatever

you feel inside. Again, let it out, otherwise, you will create problems for your body. You have to take care of yourself the best you can, and I know it's not easy.

Those of us who have been working with people with aids find that the grieving process becomes on-going. It is the same as the grieving process in war time. There are too many onslaughts to the emotional/nervous system to handle. Many times I reach out to special friends and dissolve into hysterics when it all becomes too much. It was much easier when my mother died. I felt the natural completion of her ninety-one year cycle. Though I grieved, I had no anger or rage at injustice or untimeliness. Wars and epidemics bring up tremendous frustration at the seeming unfairness of it all.

Although grieving takes time, sometimes you feel like you're in a bottomless pit. If you are still grieving after a few years, then you are wallowing in it. You need to forgive and release the other person and yourself. Remember, we don't lose anyone when they die because we never owned them in the first place.

If you are having a difficult time letting go, there are several things you can do. First of all, I suggest you do some meditations with the person who is gone. No matter what he or she thought or did while they were alive, when they leave the planet, a veil lifts and they see life very clearly. So they no longer have the fears and the beliefs that they had when they were here. If you are grieving a lot, they would probably tell you not to worry because all is well. In your meditations, ask the person for help to get you through this period, and tell him or her that you love them.

Don't judge yourself for not being with the person or doing enough for the person while he or she was alive. That's just adding guilt to your grief. Some of you use this time as an excuse for not getting on with your own life. Some of you would like to leave the planet, too. Or, for some of you, the death of someone you know and love brings up your own fear of death.

Use this time to do inner work on yourself so you can release some of your own stuff. A lot of sadness comes to the surface upon the death of a loved one. Let yourself feel the sadness. You need to get to a point where you feel safe enough to let the old pains come up. If you would allow yourself two or three days of crying, much of the sadness and guilt would disappear. If you need to, find a therapist or a group to help you feel safe enough so that you can release the emotions. Another suggestion is to say affirmations like: "*I love you and I set you free. You are free and I am free.*"

One woman at one of my workshops was having a very difficult time letting go of the anger she felt towards an aunt who was very ill. She was terrified that her aunt would pass away and she would not be able to communicate how she really felt about the past. She didn't want to speak with the aunt because she felt all choked up inside. I suggested to her that she work with a therapist, for one-on-one work can be so helpful. When we are stuck in any area, it is an act of love for ourselves to reach out for help.

There are many types of therapists all over who are experienced in these situations. You don't need to go for a long time, just a short while so that you can get through your difficult period. There are also many grief support groups. It might be helpful for you to join one because it would assist you as you go through the process.

Understanding Our Pain

Many of us live from day to day with unrelieved pain. It may be a small, inconsequential part of our lives, or it may take up a large, unbearable portion of it. But what is pain? Most of us agree that it is something we would like to be free of. Let's look at what we can learn from it. Where does it come from? What is it trying to tell us?

The dictionary defines pain as an "unpleasant or distressing sensation due to bodily injury or disorder," as well as a "mental or emotional suffering or torment." Since pain is an outgrowth of both mental and physical dis-ease, it is clear that both the mind and the body are susceptible to it.

I recently witnessed a wonderful example to illustrate this point as I watched two little girls playing in a park. The first child raised her hand to playfully slap her friend on the arm. Before she was able to connect, the other little girl said, "Ow!" The first little girl looked at her and said, "Why did you say 'Ow'? I haven't even touched you yet." To which her friend quickly replied, "Well, I *knew* it was gonna hurt." In this instance, the mental pain presumed the expected physical pain.

Pain comes to us in many forms. A scratch. A bump. A bruise. Dis-ease. Uneasy sleep. A threat. A knotty feeling in your stomach. A numbing sensation in your arm or leg. Sometimes it hurts a lot, sometimes only a little, but we know it's there. In most cases, it is trying to tell us something. At times, the message is obvious. A sour stomach experienced during the work week, but not on the weekend, may indicate a need for a job change. And many of us know the significance of the pain that occurs after a night of excessive drinking.

Whatever the message, we must remember that the human body is a wonderfully constructed piece of machinery. It tells us if there are problems but only if we are willing to listen. Unfortunately, many of us do not take or make the time to listen.

Pain is actually one of the body's "last-resort" messages to tell us that something is wrong in our lives. We're really off-track somewhere. The body is always aspiring for optimum health no matter what we do to it. However, if we abuse our bodies tremendously, we contribute to the conditions of our dis-ease.

When we first feel pain, what do we do? We usually

run to the medicine cabinet or to the drugstore, and we take a pill. In effect, we say to the body, "Shut up, I don't want to hear you." The body will quiet down for a little bit, then the whisperings return, this time a little louder. Maybe we go to the doctor for an injection or a prescription, or we do something else. At some point, we have to pay attention to what is going on because we may have a full-blown dis-ease of some sort. Even at that point, some people still want to play victim and still don't listen. Others awaken to what's going on and are willing to make changes. It's okay. We all learn in different ways.

The answers may be as simple as getting a good night's sleep, or not going out seven nights a week, or not pushing yourself at work. Allow yourself to listen to your body because it *does* want to get well. Your body wants to be healthy, and you can cooperate with it.

When I first feel pain or discomfort, I quiet myself. I trust that my Higher Power will let me know what needs to be changed in my life, so I can be free from this dis-ease. In these quiet times, I visualize the most perfect natural setting with my favorite flowers growing in abundance all around me. I can feel and smell the sweet, warm air as it blows gently across my face. I concentrate on relaxing every muscle in my body.

When I feel that I have reached a state of complete relaxation, I simply ask my Inner Wisdom, *"How am I contributing to this problem? What is it that I need to*

know? *What areas of my life are in need of change?"*
Then I let the answers pour over me. The answers may
not come at that moment but I know that they will be revealed to me soon. I know that whatever changes are
needed are the right ones for me and that I will be completely safe no matter what unfolds before me.

Sometimes you wonder how you can accomplish such
changes. "How will I live? What about the children? How
will I pay my bills?" Again, trust your Higher Power to
show you the means to live a plentiful, pain-free life.

I also suggest that you make changes one step at a time.
Lao-Tse said, *The journey of a thousand miles begins
with one step.* One small step added to another can create significant, major advancements. Once you go about
making your changes, please remember that pain does not
necessarily disappear overnight, and yet it may. It has
taken time for pain to surface; therefore, it may take some
time to recognize it is no longer needed. Be gentle to yourself. Don't gauge your progress by someone else's. You
are unique and have your own way of handling your life.
Put your trust in your Higher Self in order to free yourself of all physical and emotional pain.

Forgiveness Is the Key to Freedom

I often ask clients, "Would you rather be right or would
you rather be happy?" We all have opinions on who was
right and who was wrong according to our own percep-
tions, and we can all find ways to justify our feelings. We
want to punish others for what they did to us; however,

we are the ones running the story over and over in our own minds. It is foolish for us to punish ourselves in the present because someone hurt us in the past.

To release the past, we want to be willing to forgive, even if we don't know *how*. Forgiveness means giving up our hurtful feelings and just letting the whole thing go. A state of nonforgiveness actually destroys something within ourselves.

No matter what avenue of spirituality you follow you will usually find that forgiveness is an enormous issue at any time, but most particularly when there is an illness. When we are ill we really need to look around and see who it is we need to forgive. And usually the very person who we think we will never forgive is the one we need to forgive the most. Not forgiving someone else doesn't harm the person in the slightest, but it plays havoc with us. The issues aren't theirs; the issues are ours.

The grudges and hurts you feel have to do with forgiving yourself, not someone else. Affirm that you are totally willing to forgive everyone. *"I am willing to free myself from the past. I am willing to forgive all those who may ever have harmed me and I forgive myself for having harmed others."* If you think of anyone who may have harmed you in any way at any point in your life, bless that person with love and release him or her, then dismiss the thought.

I wouldn't be where I am today if I hadn't forgiven the

people who have hurt me. I would not want to punish myself today for what they did to me in the past. I'm not saying that it would be easy. It's just that now I can look back at that stuff and say, "Oh yes, that's something that happened." However, I don't live there anymore. It is not the same thing as condoning their behavior.

If you feel ripped-off by another, know that nobody can take anything from you that is rightfully yours. If it belongs to you, it will return to you at the right time. If something doesn't come back to you, it wasn't meant to. You need to accept it and go on with your life.

To become free, you need to get out of your self-righteous resentment and off your *pity pot*. I love this expression, which originated with Alcoholics Anonymous, because it is such a wonderful, accurate description. When you are sitting on your *pity pot*, you are this helpless person who has no power at all. In order to have power, you have to stand on your own two feet and take responsibility.

Take a moment and close your eyes and imagine a beautiful stream of water in front of you. Take the old painful experience, the hurt, and the unforgiveness, and put the whole incident in the stream. See it begin to dissolve and drift downstream until it totally dissipates and disappears. Do this as often as you can.

This is a time for compassion and healing. Go within and connect with that part of yourself that knows how to heal. You are incredibly capable. Be willing to go to new levels to find capabilities of which you were not aware, not to just cure dis-ease, but to truly heal yourself on all possible levels. To make yourself whole in the deepest sense of the word. To accept every part of yourself and every experience you have ever had, and to know that it is all part of the tapestry of your life this time around.

I love *Emmanuel's Book*. There is a passage in it which has a good message.

The question to Emmanuel is:
"How do we experience painful circumstances without becoming embittered by them?'

And Emmanuel's reply is:
"By seeing them as lessons and not as retribution. Trust life, my friends. However far afield life seems to take you, this trip is necessary. You have come to traverse a wide terrain of experience in order to verify where truth lies and where your distortion is in that terrain. You will then be able to return to your home center, your soul self, refreshed and wiser."

If only we could understand that all of our so-called problems are just opportunities for us to grow and to change, and that most of them come from the vibrations that we have been giving off! All we really need to do is change the way we think, be willing to dissolve the resentment, and be willing to forgive.

PART THREE

Loving Yourself

Can you remember the last time you were in love? Your heart went ahhhh. *It was such a wonderful feeling. It's the same thing with loving yourself except that you will never leave. Once you have your love for yourself, it's with you for the rest of your life, so you want to make it the best relationship you can have.*

Chapter 8

How to Love Yourself

*When you forgive and let go, not only
does a huge weight drop off your
shoulders, but the doorway to your
own self-love opens.*

For many of you who have been working on loving yourselves and for those of you who are just beginning, I am
going to explore some ways to help you learn how to love
yourselves. I call it my *Ten Steps*, and I have sent thousands of people this list over the years.

Loving yourself is a wonderful adventure; it's like learning to fly. Imagine if we all had the power to fly at will?
How exciting it would be! Let's begin to love ourselves
now.

Many of us seem to suffer from a lack of self-esteem at
one level or another. It is very difficult for us to love ourselves because we have all these so-called faults inside us
that we feel make it impossible to love ourselves exactly
as we are. We usually make loving ourselves conditional,
and then when we are involved in relationships, we make
loving the other person conditional also. We've all heard
that we really can't love someone else until we love ourselves. So now that we have seen the barriers we have set
up for ourselves, how do we catapult to the next step.

10 Ways to Love Yourself

1. Probably the most important key is to **stop criticizing yourself**. I talked about criticism in chapter five. If we tell ourselves that we are okay, no matter what is going on, we can make changes in our lives easily. It is when we make ourselves *bad* that we have great difficulty. We all change—everyone. Every day is a new day, and we do things a little differently than we did the day before. Our ability to adapt and flow with the process of life is our power.

Those who have come from dysfunctional homes often have become super-responsible and have gotten in the habit of judging themselves unmercifully. They have grown up amidst tension and anxiety. The message they get as children of dysfunctional homes is: "There must be something wrong with me." Think for a moment about the words you use when scolding yourself. Some of the phrases people tell me are: stupid, bad boy, bad girl, useless, careless, dumb, ugly, worthless, sloppy, dirty, et cetera. Are these the same words you use now when describing yourself?

2. There is a tremendous need to build self-worth and value in ourselves, because when we feel *not good enough*, we find ways to keep ourselves miserable. We create illness or pain in our bodies; we procrastinate about things that would benefit us; we mistreat our bodies with food, alcohol, and drugs.

We are all insecure in some ways because we are human. Let us learn not to pretend that we are perfect. Having to be perfect only puts immense pressure on ourselves, and it prevents us from looking at areas of our lives that need healing. Instead, we could discover our creative distinctions, our individualities, and appreciate ourselves for the qualities that set us apart from others. Each one of us has a unique role to play on this earth, and when we are critical of ourselves, we obscure it.

2. We must also **stop scaring ourselves**. Many of us terrorize ourselves with frightful thoughts and make situations worse than they are. We take a small problem and make it into a big monster. It's a terrible way to live, always expecting the worst out of life.

PAST

How many of you go to bed at night creating the worst possible scenario of a problem? That is like a little child who imagines monsters under the bed and then gets terrified. It's no wonder you can't sleep. As a child you needed your parent to come and soothe you. Now as an adult you know you have the ability to soothe yourself.

People who are ill do this a lot. Often they visualize the worst or they are immediately planning their funerals. They give their power to the media and see themselves as statistics.

You may also do this in relationships. Someone doesn't call and you immediately decide that you are totally unlovable and you'll never have another relationship again. You feel abandoned and rejected.

You do the same thing with your job. Someone makes a remark at work, and you begin to think you're going to be fired. You build these paralyzing thoughts in your mind. Remember, these frightening thoughts are negative affirmations.

If you find yourself habitually reviewing a negative thought or situation in your mind, find an image of something you really would like to replace it with. It could be a beautiful view, or a sunset, flowers, a sport, or anything you love. Use that image as your *switch-to* image every time you find that you are scaring yourself. Say to yourself, "No, I'm not going to think about that anymore. I'm going to think about sunsets, or roses, or Paris, or yachts, or waterfalls," whatever your image is. If you keep doing this, you will eventually break the habit. Again, it takes practice.

3. Another way is **be gentle and kind and patient with yourself.** Oren Arnold humorously wrote, *"Dear God—I pray for patience. And I want it right now!* Patience is a very powerful tool. Most of us suffer from the expectation of immediate gratification. We must have it now. We don't have the patience to wait for anything. We get irritable if we have to wait in lines or are stuck in traffic. We want all the answers and all the goodies right now. Too often, we make other people's lives miserable by our own impatience. Impatience is a resistance to learning. We want the answers without learning the lesson or doing the steps that are necessary.

Think of your mind as if it were a garden. To begin with, a garden is a patch of dirt. You may have a lot of brambles of self-hatred and rocks of despair, anger, and worry. An old tree, called fear, needs pruning. Once you get some of these things out of the way, and the soil is in good shape, you add some seeds or little plants of joy and prosperity. The sun shines down on it, and you water it and give it nutrients and loving attention.

At first, not much seems to be happening. But you don't stop, you keep taking care of your garden. If you are patient, the garden will grow and blossom. The same with your mind—you select the thoughts that will be nurtured, and with patience they grow and contribute to creating the garden of experiences you want.

We All Make Mistakes

It's okay to make mistakes while you are learning. As I said, so many of you are cursed with perfectionism. You won't give yourselves a chance to really learn anything new because if you don't do it perfectly in the first three minutes, you assume you are not good enough.

Anything you are going to learn takes time. When you first begin doing something, it usually doesn't feel right. To show you what I mean, take a moment right now and clasp your hands together. There is no right or wrong way to do this. Clasp your hands and notice which thumb is on top. Now open your hands and then clasp your hands again with the other thumb on top. It probably feels strange, odd, maybe even wrong. Clasp them again the first way, then the second, and the first again, and the second way and hold it. How does it feel? Not so odd. Not so bad. You're getting used to it. Maybe you can even learn to do it both ways.

It's the same when we are doing something a new way. It may feel different, and we immediately judge it. Yet, with a little bit of practice, it can become normal and natural. We're not going to love ourselves totally in one day, but we can love ourselves a little bit more every day.

Each day, we give ourselves a little bit more love, and in two or three months, we will have come so much further in loving ourselves.

So mistakes are your stepping stones. They are valuable because they are your teachers. Don't punish yourself for making a mistake. If you are willing to learn and grow from the mistake, then it serves as a step toward fulfillment in your life.

Some of us have been working on ourselves for a very long time and wonder why we still have issues that come up for us. We need to keep reinforcing what we know, not resisting by throwing our hands up in the air and saying, "What's the use?" As we learn new ways, we need to be gentle and kind to ourselves. Remember the garden above. When the negative weeds grow, pluck them out as quickly as you can.

4. We must **learn to be kind to our minds**. Let's not hate ourselves for having negative thoughts. We can think of our thoughts as *building* us up rather than *beating* us up. We don't have to blame ourselves for negative experiences. We can learn from these experiences. Being kind to ourselves means we stop all blame, all guilt, all punishment, and all pain.

Relaxation can help us as well. Relaxation is absolutely essential for tapping into the Power within, because if you are tense and frightened, you shut off your energy. It only takes a few minutes a day to allow the body and the mind to let go and relax. At any moment you can take a few deep breaths, close your eyes, and release whatever tension you're carrying. As you exhale, become centered and say to yourself silently: *"I love you. All is well."* You will notice how much calmer you feel. You are building messages that say you don't have to go through life tense and frightened all the time.

Meditate on a Daily Basis

I also recommend quieting your mind and listening to your own inner wisdom. Our society has made meditation into something mysterious and difficult to achieve, and yet meditation is one of the oldest and simplest processes there is. All we need to do is get into a relaxed state and repeat silently to ourselves words like *love* or *peace* or anything meaningful to us. *OM* is an ancient sound that I use at my workshops and it seems to work very well. We could even repeat: *I love myself*, or *I forgive myself*, or *I am forgiven*. Then listen for a while.

Some people think that if they meditate, they have to stop their minds from thinking. We really can't stop the mind, but we can slow down our thoughts and let them flow through. Some people sit with a pad and pencil and write down their negative thoughts because they seem to dissipate more easily. If we can get to a state where we are watching our thoughts float by—"Oh, there's a fear thought, and some anger, now there is a love thought, and now a disaster, there's an abandonment thought, a joy thought"—and don't give them importance, we begin to use our tremendous power wisely.

You can begin meditation anywhere and allow it to become a habit. Think of meditation as focusing on your

Higher Power. You become connected with yourself and your inner wisdom. You can do it in whatever form you like. Some people go into a kind of meditation while they are jogging or walking. Again, don't make yourself wrong for doing it differently. I love to get on my knees in the garden and dig in the dirt. It's a great meditation for me.

Visualize Optimistic Outcomes

Visualization is also very important, and there are many techniques you can use. Dr. Carl Simonton, in his book, *Getting Well Again*, recommends a lot of visualization techniques for people with cancer and they often yield excellent results.

With visualization you create a clear, positive image that enhances your affirmation. Many of you have written to me about the kinds of visualizations you do along with your affirmations. The important thing to remember about visualizations is that they must be compatible with the kind of person you are. Otherwise, your visualizations will not work.

For instance, a woman with cancer pictured the *good killer cells* in her body attacking the cancer and killing it. At the end of the visualization, she doubted whether she had done it correctly and didn't feel that it was working for her. So I asked her, "Are you a killer person?" I personally don't feel good about creating a war in my body. I suggested that she change her visualization to one that was a little more gentle. I think it's better to use images like the sun melting the sick cells, or a magician transforming them with his magic wand. When I had my

cancer, I used the visualization of cool, clear water wash-
ing the dis-eased cells out of my body. We need to do
visualizations that are not so offensive to us on the subconscious level.

Those of us who have family or friends who are sick
do them an injustice by continually seeing them sick.
Visualize them well. Send them good vibrations.
However, remember that getting well is really up to them.
There are many good audiotapes with guided visualizations and meditations that you can give them to help them
through this process if they are open. If not, just send
them love.

Everyone can visualize. Describing your home, having
a sexual fantasy, imagining what you would do to a person who hurt you are all visualizations. It is amazing what
the mind can do.

5. The next step is to **praise yourself**. Criticism breaks
down the inner spirit, and praise builds it up. Acknowledge your Power, your God self. We are all expressions of the Infinite Intelligence. When you berate
yourself, you belittle the Power that created you. Begin
with little things. Tell yourself that you are wonderful. If
you do it once and then stop, it doesn't work. Keep at it,
even if it's one minute at a time. Believe me, it does get
easier. The next time you do something new, or different, or something you are just learning and you're not too
adept at it, be there for yourself.

It was a big thrill the first time I spoke at the Church
of Religious Science in New York. I remember it vividly.
It was a Friday noon meeting. People wrote questions and
put them in a basket for me, the speaker. I brought the

basket to the podium and answered the questions and did a small treatment after each. After I finished, I walked away from the podium and said to myself, "Louise, you were fantastic considering this was the first time out. By the time you do this about six times, you are going to be a pro." I didn't berate myself and say, "Oh, you forgot to say this or that." I didn't want to have the second time be something that would frighten me.

If I beat myself up the first time, I would beat myself up the second time, and I would dread speaking in the end. After a couple of hours, I thought of what I could change to improve. I never made myself wrong. I was very careful to praise myself and congratulate myself for being wonderful. By the time I had conducted six meetings, I was a pro. I think we can apply this method in all areas of our lives. I continued speaking at the meetings for quite some time. It was a wonderful training ground because it taught me how to think on my feet.

Allow yourself to accept *good* whether you think you deserve it or not. I've discussed how believing that we are not deserving is our unwillingness to accept good in our lives. It's what stops us from having what we want. How could we say anything good about ourselves if we think we don't deserve to be good.

Think about the laws of deserving in your home. Did you feel good enough, smart enough, tall enough, pretty enough, whatever? And what do you have to live for? You know you are here for a reason, and it's not to buy a new car every few years. What are you willing to do to fulfill yourself? Are you willing to do affirmations, visualizations, treatments? Are you willing to forgive? Are you willing to meditate? How much mental effort are you willing to exert to change your life and make it the life you want?

6. Loving yourself means supporting yourself. Reach out to friends and allow them to help you. You really are being strong when you ask for help when you need it. So many of you have learned to be so self-reliant and self-sufficient. You can't ask for help because your ego won't let you. Instead of trying to do it all yourself and then getting angry at yourself because you can't make it, try asking for help next time.

There are support groups in every city. There are 12-Step Programs for almost every problem, and in some areas there are healing circles and church-affiliated organizations. If you can't find what you want, you can start your own group. It's not as scary as you might think. Gather together two or three friends who have the same issues that you have, and set up a few guidelines to follow. If you do it with love in your heart, your little group will grow. People will be attracted like a magnet. Don't worry if it starts to grow and your meeting space gets too small. The Universe always provides. If you don't know what to do, write to my office, and we'll send you guidelines on how to conduct a group. You really can be there for each other.

I started *The Hayride* in Los Angeles in 1985 with six men with aids in my living room. We didn't know what we were going to do about this intense crisis. I told them we weren't going to sit around playing "ain't it awful" because we already knew that. We did what we could on a positive level to support each other. We're still meeting today, and we have about 200 people coming every Wednesday night to West Hollywood Park.

It's an extraordinary group for people with aids, and everyone is welcome. People come from all over the world to see how this group functions and because they feel supported. It's not only me, it's the group. Everyone contributes to making it effective. We meditate and do visualizations. We network and share information about alternative therapies and the latest medical methods. There are energy tables at one end of the room where people can lie down, and others share healing energies by laying on hands or praying for them. We have Science of Mind Practitioners they can talk to. At the end we sing and hug one another. We want people to go out feeling better than they came in, and sometimes people receive a positive lift that lasts for several days.

Support groups have become the new social form and they are very effectual tools in this complex day and age. Many "new thought" churches such as Unity and Religious Science have ongoing weekly support groups. Many groups are listed in new age magazines and newspapers.

Networking is so important. It sparks you and gets you going. I suggest that people who have similar ideas share time with one another on a regular basis.

When people work together on a common goal, they bring their pain, confusion, anger, or whatever, and come together, not to moan, but to find a way to go beyond, to rise above, and grow up in a way.

If you are very dedicated, very self-disciplined, and very spiritual, you can do a lot of work on yourself by yourself. When you are with a group of people doing the same thing, you can make quantum leaps because you learn from one another. Every single person in the group is a teacher. So if you have issues that need working on, I would suggest, if possible, that you get into a group of some sort where you can work them through.

7. **Love your negatives.** They are all part of your creation, just as we are all part of God's creation. The Intel- *God*
ligence that created us doesn't hate us because we make mistakes or get angry at our children. This Intelligence *God* knows that we are doing the best we can and loves all of Its creation, as we can love ours. You and I have all made negative choices, and if we keep punishing ourselves for them, it becomes a habit pattern and we'll find it very tiresome to let them go and move on to more positive choices.

If you keep repeating, "I hate my job. I hate my house. I hate my illness. I hate this relationship. I hate this. I hate that," very little new good can come into your life.

No matter what negative situation you are in, it's there for a reason; otherwise you wouldn't have it in your life. Dr. John Harrison, the author of *Love Your Disease*, says that patients are never to be condemned for having multiple operations or illnesses. Actually, patients can congratulate themselves for finding a safe way to have their needs met. We have to understand that whatever issue or problem we have, we contributed to creating it in order to handle certain situations. Once we realize this, then we can find a positive way to fulfill our needs.

Sometimes people with cancer or other terminal illnesses have such a hard time saying "no" to an authoritative figure in their life, that on an unconscious level they will create a major dis-ease to say "no" for them. I knew a woman who, when she realized the illness she was creating for herself was just to be able to refuse her father's demands, decided to begin to live for herself for once. She began to say "no" to him. And while it was difficult for her at first, as she continued to stand up for herself she was delighted to find herself getting well.

Whatever our negative patterns are, we can learn to fulfill those needs in more positive ways. That's why it's so important to ask yourself the question, "What is the payoff from this experience? What am I getting that's positive?" We don't like to answer that question. However if we really look within and are honest with ourselves we will find that answer.

Perhaps your answer would be, "It's the only time I get loving attention from my spouse." Once realized, you can begin to look for more positive ways to achieve this.

Humor is another potent tool—it helps us release and lighten up during stressful experiences. At the *Hayride*, we set time aside for jokes. Sometimes we have a guest speaker called the "the laugh lady". She has a contagious laugh and puts everyone on a laughter cycle. We can't always take ourselves too seriously, and laughter is very healing. I also recommend watching old comedies such as those of Laurel and Hardy when you are feeling low or down.

When I did private counseling I would do my best to get people to begin to laugh at their problems. When we can see our lives as a stage play with soap opera and drama and comedy, we get a better perspective and we are on the way to healing. Humor enables us to pull back from the experience and to see it in a larger perspective.

8. Take care of your body. Think of it as this marvelous house in which you live for a while. You would love your house and take care of it, wouldn't you? So, watch what you put into your body. Drug and alcohol abuse is so prevalent because they are two of the most popular methods of escape. If you are into drugs it doesn't mean you are a bad person; it means you haven't found a more positive way of fulfilling your needs.

Drugs beckon to us: "Come and play with me, and we'll have a good time." It's true. They can make you feel wonderful. However, they alter your reality so much, and although it isn't evident at first, you have to pay a terrible price in the end. After taking drugs for a while, your health deteriorates immensely, and you feel awful most of the time. Drugs affect your immune system, which can lead to numerous physical ailments. Also, after repeated use, you develop an addiction, and you have to wonder what made you start taking drugs in the first place. Peer pressure may have compelled you to take them in the beginning, but continued and repeated use is another story.

I've yet to meet anyone who really loves him or herself

and who is hooked on drugs. We use drugs and alcohol to escape our childhood feelings of not being good enough and when they wear off, we feel worse than before. Then we usually have a load of guilt, too. We have to know that it's safe to feel our feelings and acknowledge them. The feelings pass, they don't stay.

Stuffing food into our bodies is another way to hide our love. We can't live without food because it fuels our bodies and helps to create new cells. Even though we may know the basics of good nutrition, often we still use food and diets to punish ourselves and create obesity.

We've become a nation of junk food addicts. We have been on what I call the *Great American Diet* for decades, filling ourselves with processed foods of every sort. We've allowed the food companies and their advertising gimmicks to influence our eating habits. Doctors aren't even taught nutrition in medical schools, unless they take it as an extracurricular subject. Most of what we consider conventional medicine, at the moment, concentrates on drugs and surgery, so if we really want to learn about nutrition, it's an issue that we must take into our own hands. It's an act of loving ourselves to become aware of what we put into our mouths and how it makes us feel.

If you eat lunch, and an hour later, you start feeling sleepy, you might ask yourself, "What did I eat?" You may have consumed something that isn't good for your body at that particular time. Start noticing what gives you energy and what depletes you and brings you down. You can do it by trial and error, or you could find a good nutritionist who can answer some of your questions.

Remember that what's right for one person isn't necessarily right for another—our bodies are different. A macrobiotic diet is wonderful for many people. So is Harvey and Marilyn Diamond's *Fit For Life* method. They are totally different concepts, and yet they both work. Every body is different from every other body, so we can't say that only one method works. You have to find out which way works best for you.

Find exercise that you enjoy, that is fun to do. Create a positive mental attitude about your exercise. Often, you create obstacles in your bodies primarily as a result of what you absorb from other people. Again, you need to forgive yourself and stop putting anger and resentment into your body if you want to create changes. Combining affirmations with your exercise is a way to reprogram negative concepts about your body and its shape.

We are in a time now where new technologies for health are multiplying, and we are learning to combine some ancient healing methods such as Ayurvedic medicine with sound wave technology. I have been studying how sound can stimulate our brain waves and accelerate our learning and healing. There is research that shows that we can cure illness by mentally changing our DNA structure. I think between now and the end of the century, we are going to explore a range of possibilities that will be enormously beneficial to much of the populace.

9. I often emphasize the importance of **mirror work** in order to find out the cause of an issue that keeps us from loving ourselves. There are several ways that you can practice mirror work. I like to look in the mirror the first thing in the morning and say: *"I love you. What can I do for you today? How can I make you happy?"* Listen to your inner voice, and start following through with what you hear. You may not get any messages to begin with because you're so used to scolding yourself, and you don't know how to respond with a kind, loving thought.

If something unpleasant happens to you during the day, go to the mirror and say: *"I love you anyway."* Events come and go, but the love that you have for yourself is constant, and it is the most important quality you possess in your life. If something wonderful happens, go to the mirror and say, "Thank you." Acknowledge yourself for creating this wonderful experience.

You can forgive in the mirror, too. Forgive yourself and forgive others. You can talk to other people in the mirror, especially when you are afraid to talk to them in person. You can clean up old issues with people—parents, bosses, doctors, children, lovers. You can say all sorts of things that you would be afraid to say otherwise, and remember to end by asking them for their love and approval because that is what you really want.

People who have problems loving themselves are almost always people who are not willing to forgive because not forgiving shuts that particular door. When we forgive and let go, not only does a huge weight drop off our shoulders, but the doorway to our own self-love opens up. People will say, "Oh, such a load has dropped off!" Well, of course it has, because we've been carrying this burden forever. Dr. John Harrison states that forgiveness of both the self and the parents, coupled with the release of past hurts, cures more illness than any antibiotic ever could.

It takes a lot to make children stop loving their parents, but when they do, it takes even more for them to forgive them. When we won't forgive, when we won't let go, we're binding ourselves to the past, and when we are stuck in the past, we cannot live in present time, and if we are not living in the present, how can we create our glorious future? Old garbage from the past just creates more garbage for the future.

Affirmations performed in front of a mirror are advantageous because you learn the truth of your existence. When you do an affirmation and you immediately hear a negative response such as, "Who are you kidding? It can't be true. You don't deserve that," then you have received a gift to use. You cannot make the changes you want until you are willing to see what is holding you back. The negative response you have just discovered is like a gift in that it becomes the key to freedom. Turn that negative response into a positive affirmation such as: *"I now deserve all good. I allow good experiences to fill my life."* Repeat the new affirmation until it does become a new part of your life.

I have also seen families change enormously when just one person does affirmations. Many people at the *Hayride* come from estranged families. Their parents literally will not talk to them. I've had them repeat the affirmation, *"I have wonderful, loving, warm, open communication with every member of my family, including my mother,"* or whoever the problem person was. Every time that person or the family comes to mind, I suggest that they go to the mirror and say the affirmation over and over again. It is amazing to see the parents actually show up at the meeting three, or six, or nine months later.

10. Finally, **love yourself** *now*—don't wait until you get it right. Dissatisfaction with yourself is a habit pattern. If you can be satisfied with yourself now, if you can love and approve of yourself now, then when good comes into your life, you will be able to enjoy it. Once you learn to love yourself, you can begin to love and accept other people.

We can't change other people, so leave them alone. We spend a lot of energy trying to make others different. If we used half that energy on ourselves, we could make ourselves different, and when *we* are different, others respond differently to us.

You can't learn life for another person. Everyone has to learn his or her particular lessons. All you can do is learn for yourself, and loving yourself is the first step, so you are not brought down by other people's destructive behaviors. If you are in a situation where you are with a really negative person who doesn't want to change, you need to love yourself enough to move away from that.

One woman at one of my lectures told me that her husband was very negative, and she didn't want him to be a bad influence on her two little children. I suggested that she start affirming that her husband was a wonderful, supportive man who really is working on himself and is bringing out his best qualities. I told her to affirm what she would like to have happen, and every time he was negative, simply run the affirmation through her mind. However, if the relationship continued negatively no matter what affirmations she said, then that might be an answer in itself—the relationship simply wouldn't work.

Because of the increasing divorce rate in our country, I think a question that many women need to ask themselves before they have children is: "Am I really willing to support these children totally on my own?" Being a single parent has become more and more the norm, and it's almost always the woman who acquires the added responsibility of raising children by herself. There was a time when marriages lasted a lifetime, but times have changed, so it's definitely a situation to be considered.

Far too often, we stay in abusive relationships and allow ourselves to be put down. What we are saying is, "I'm not worth loving, so I will stay here and accept this behavior because I must deserve it and I am sure nobody else would want me."

I know that I sound simplistic and repeat the same expressions over and over again, but I truly do believe that the quickest way to change any problem is to love who we are. It is amazing how the loving vibrations we send out will attract to us people who are loving.

Unconditional love is the goal I think we have come here to attain. It begins with self-acceptance and self-love.

You are not here to please other people or to live your lives their way. You can only live it your own way and walk your own pathway. You have come to fulfill yourself and express love on the deepest level. You are here to learn and grow and to absorb and project compassion and understanding. When you leave the planet, you don't take your relationship or your automobile or your bank account or your job with you. The only thing you take is your capacity to love!

Chapter 9

Loving the Child Within

*If you can't get close to other people,
it is because you don't know how to
be close to your own inner child. The
child in you is scared and hurting. Be
there for your child.*

One of the core issues that we want to begin to explore is healing the forgotten child within. Most of us have ignored our inner child for far too long.

It doesn't matter how old you are, there is a little child within you who needs love and acceptance. If you're a woman, no matter how self-reliant you are, you have a little girl who's very tender and needs help; and if you are a man, no matter how macho you are, you still have a little boy inside of you who craves warmth and affection.

Every age that you have been is within you—within your consciousness and memory. As children, when something went wrong, you tended to believe that there was something wrong with you. Children develop the idea that if they could only do it right, then parents or whoever would love them, and they wouldn't beat them or punish them.

So whenever the child wants something and doesn't get it, he or she believes, "I'm not good enough. I'm defective." And, as we grow older, we reject certain parts of ourselves.

At this point in our lives—right now—we need to begin to make ourselves whole and accept every part of who we are—the part that did all the stupid things, the part that was funny looking, the part that was scared, the part that was very foolish and silly, the part that had egg on its face. Every single part of ourselves.

I think that we often turn off or tune out around the age of five. We make that decision because we think that there is something wrong with us, and we're not going to have anything to do with the child anymore.

There is a parent inside, as well. You have a child and you have a parent, and most of the time, the parent scolds the child, almost on a nonstop basis. If you listen to your inner dialogue, you can hear the scolding. You can hear the parent tell you what you are doing wrong or how you are not good enough.

Consequently, we begin a war with ourselves, and we start to criticize ourselves the way our parents have been criticizing us. "You're stupid. You're not good enough. You don't do it right. Screwed up again!" It becomes a habit pattern. When we become adults, most of us totally ignore the child within us, or we criticize the child in the same way we used to be criticized. We continue the pattern over and over again.

I once heard John Bradshaw, author of several marvelous books on healing the inner child, say that each of us has 25,000 hours of parent tapes within us by the time we are adults. How many hours of those tapes, do you think, are telling you how wonderful you are? How much says that you are loved or that you are bright and intelligent? Or that you could do anything you wanted to and would grow up to be the greatest person? In reality, how many hours of those tapes are saying "No, No, No," in all its many forms?

It's no wonder we say *no* to ourselves or *should* all the time. We are responding to those old tapes. However, they are only tapes and are not the reality of your being. They are not the truth of your existence. They are just tapes you carry within, and they can be erased or rerecorded.

Every time you say that you are scared, realize it is the child in you who's scared. The grown-up really isn't afraid, yet the adult isn't being there for the child. The adult and the child need to develop a relationship with each other. Talk to each other about everything you do. I know it may sound silly, but it works. Let the child know that no matter what happens, you will never turn away or run away. You will always be there for it and love it.

For instance, if, when you were very young, you had a bad experience with a dog; that is, maybe it scared you or even bit you, the little child inside could still be frightened of dogs even though now you are a great, big adult. You may see a dog on the street that is teeny, but the little child inside you reacts in a total panic. It says, "DOG!!! I'm going to be hurt!" This is a wonderful opportunity for the parent inside of you to say to the child, "It's okay, I'm grown up now. I will take care of you. I won't let the dog hurt you. You don't have to be frightened anymore." Start parenting your own child in this way.

Healing the Hurts of the Past

I have found that working with the inner child is most valuable in helping to heal the hurts of the past. We are not always in touch with the feelings of the frightened little child within us. If your childhood was full of fear and battling, and you now mentally beat yourself up, you are continuing to treat your inner child in much the same way. The child inside, however, has no place to go. You need to go beyond your parents' limitations. You need to connect with the little lost child inside. He or she needs to know that you care.

Take a moment now and tell your child that you care, "I care. I love you. I really love you." Maybe you've been saying this to the big person, the adult inside you. So start talking to the little child. Visualize that you are taking him or her by the hand and go everywhere together for a few days, and see what wonderfully joyous experiences you can have.

You need to communicate with that part of yourself. What are the messages you want to hear? Sit down quietly, close your eyes, and talk to your child. If you haven't talked to her or him in 62 years, it may take a few times before the child will believe that you really want to talk to it. Be persistent: *"I want to talk to you. I want to see you. I want to love you."* You will eventually connect. You may see the child inside you, you may feel it, or you may hear it.

One of the first statements that you can make when you first talk to your child is an apology. Say you are sorry that you haven't talked to it in all these years, or that you are sorry for scolding it for so long. Tell the child that you want to make up for all the time spent apart from one another. Ask it how you can make it happy. Ask the child what frightens him or her. Ask how you can help, and ask what it wants from you.

Start out with simple questions; you will get the answers. *"What can I do to make you happy? What would you like today?"* For instance, you can say to the child, "I want to jog, what do you want to do?" He or she may answer, "Go to the beach." The communication will have begun. Be consistent. If you can take just a few moments a day to begin to connect with the little person inside of you, life is going to be a lot better.

Communicating with Your Inner Child

Some of you may already be doing inner-child work. There are many books on the subject, and many workshops and lectures are given about it. I've listed some books at the end for further study.

Self-Parenting, by John Pollard III, is excellent, and it's filled with wonderful exercises and activities that you can do with your inner child. If you are serious about doing practical work with your inner child, I recommend that you pick up this book. As I said before, there is a lot of help offered in this area. You are not alone and helpless, but you need to reach out and ask for help so that you can get assistance.

Another suggestion I have is to find a photograph of yourself as a child. Really look at the photograph. Do you see a miserable little kid? Do you see a happy child? Whatever you see, connect with it. If you see a frightened child, ask it why it was frightened, and start doing something to make it feel better. Find several photos of your younger self, and talk to the child in each photo.

It helps to talk to your child in the mirror. If you had a nickname as a child, use that name. Have a box of tissues handy. I suggest that you sit down in front of the mirror because if you are standing, as soon as it gets difficult, you will run out the door. Instead, sit down with your box of tissues, and start talking.

Another exercise you can do is to communicate through writing. Again, lots of information will surface. Use two different colored pens or felt markers. With one colored pen in your dominant hand, write a question. With the other colored pen in your nondominant hand, let your child write the answer. It's a very fascinating exercise. When you are writing the question, the adult thinks it knows the answer, but by the time you pick up the pen with the awkward hand, the answer often comes out quite differently than expected.

You can draw together, too. Many of you probably loved drawing and coloring when you were little children until you were told to be neat and not to draw out of the lines. So begin drawing again. Use your nondominant hand to draw a picture about an event that just happened. Notice how you feel. Ask your child a question, and just let it draw with the nondominant hand and see what it shows.

If you can get together with others in small core groups, or support groups, you can work on these ideas together. You can all let your inner children draw pictures, then you can sit around and carefully discuss what the pictures mean. The information you receive can be surprisingly insightful.

Play with your little child. Do things that your child likes to do. When you were little, what did you really like to do? When was the last time you did it? Too often, the parent inside us stops us from having fun because it's not the adult thing to do. So, take the time to play and have fun. Do the silly things you did when you were young, such as jumping in piles of leaves and running under the hose spray. Watch other children at play. It will bring back memories of the games you played.

If you want more fun in your life, make the connection with your inner child and come from that space of spontaneity and joy. I promise that you will start having more fun in your life.

Were you welcomed as a child? Were your parents really glad you were born? Were they delighted with your sexuality, or did they want the opposite sex? Did you *feel* you were wanted as a child? Was there a celebration when you arrived? Whatever the responses are, welcome your child now. Create a celebration. Tell it all the wonderful things you would tell a little baby who was welcomed into its new life.

What is it you always wanted your parents to tell you when you were a child? What was it they never said that you wanted to hear? All right, tell your child that very thing. Tell it to your child every day for a month while looking in the mirror. See what happens.

If you had alcoholic or abusive parents as a child, you can meditate and visualize them as sober, gentle people. Give your child what it wants. It has probably been deprived for too long. Start visualizing the sort of life you would like to have with this child. When the child feels safe and happy, it can trust you. Ask: *"What do I need to do so that you can trust me?"* Again, you will be amazed at some of the answers.

If you had parents who were not loving at all, and it's really hard for you to relate to them, find a picture of what you think a loving father or a loving mother looks like. Put the pictures of the loving parents around the photo of yourself as a child. Create some new images. Re-write your childhood if you must.

The beliefs that you learned when you were little are still inside the child. If your parents had rigid ideas, and you're very hard on yourself or tend to build walls, your child is probably still following your parents' rules. If you continue to pick on yourself for every mistake, it must be very scary for your inner child to wake up in the morning. "What is she or he going to yell at me about today?"

What our parents did to us is in the past was their consciousness. We are the parents now. We are using our consciousness. If you are still refusing to take care of the little child, you are stuck in self-righteous resentment. Invariably, it means that there is still someone to forgive. So what is it you haven't forgiven yourself for? What do you need to let go of? Well, whatever it is, just let it go.

If we are not giving the child praise and attention now, our parents aren't the blame. They were doing what they thought was right in that particular space and time. However, now, in the present moment, we know what we can do to nourish the child within us.

Those of you who had or have a pet know what it's like to come home and have the pet greet you at the door. It

doesn't care what you are wearing. It doesn't care how old you are or if you have wrinkles or how much money you made today. The animal only cares that you're there. It loves you unconditionally. Do that for yourself. Be thrilled that you are alive and that you are here. You are the one person you are going to live with forever. Until you are willing to love the inner child, it's very hard for other people to love you. Accept yourself unconditionally and open-heartedly.

I find that it is often very helpful to create a meditation to make your child feel safe. Since I was a child of incest, I invented a wonderful imagery for my little girl.

First of all, she has a fairy godmother who looks just like Billie Burke in *The Wizard of Oz* because that's what really appeals to her. I know that when I'm not with her, she is with her fairy godmother, and she is always safe. She also lives in a penthouse way up high, with a door-man and two large dogs, so she knows that no one will ever hurt her again. When I can make her feel absolutely safe, then I, as the adult, can help her to release the pain-ful experiences.

There was a time recently when I got off-center and cried for two hours. I realized that the little child in me suddenly felt very hurt and unprotected. I had to tell her that she wasn't bad or wrong. Rather, that she was react-ing to something that had happened. So as quickly as I was able to, I did some affirmations and meditated, knowing that there was a Power far greater that would support and love me. After that, the little girl didn't feel so afraid and alone.

I'm also a great believer in teddy bears. When you were very little, often your teddy bear was your very first friend. It was your confidante because you could tell all your troubles and secrets to it, and it never snitched on you. It was always there for you. Take your teddy bear out of the closet now, and let your child have it once again.

It would also be marvelous for hospitals to supply teddy bears in all the beds, so that when the little child in us feels alone and frightened in the middle of the night, he or she can have a teddy bear to hug.

The Many Parts of You

Relationships are wonderful, marriages are wonderful, but the reality is, they are all temporary. However, your relationship with *you* is eternal. It goes on forever. Love the family within you—the child, the parent, and the youth-in-between.

Remember that there is a teen inside you, too. Welcome the teenager. Work with the teen as you work with the little child. What were all the difficulties that you went through as a teenager? Ask your teen the questions that you ask your child. Help the teenager through the intimidating episodes and apprehensive moments of puberty and beyond. Make these times okay. Learn to love your teen as you learn to love your child.

We can't love and accept each other until we love and accept that lost child within us. How old is the little lost child within you? Three, four, five? Usually, the child is less than five years old because that is generally when the child shuts down out of the need to survive.

Take your child by the hand, and love it. Create a wonderful life for you and your child. Say to yourself: *"I'm willing to learn to love my child. I am willing."* The Universe will respond. You will find ways to heal your child and yourself. If we want to heal, we must be willing to feel our feelings and move through them to the other side for the healing. Remember, our Higher Power is always available to support us in our efforts.

No matter what your early childhood was like, the best or the worst, you and only you are in charge of your life now. You can spend your time blaming your parents or your early environment, but all that accomplishes is to keep you stuck in victim patterns. It never helps you get the good you say you want.

Love is the biggest eraser I know. Love erases even the deepest and most painful memories because love goes deeper than anything else. If your mental images of the past are very strong, and you keep affirming, "It's all their fault," you stay stuck. Do you want a life of pain or one of joy? The choice and power are always within you. Look into your eyes, and love you and the little child within.

Chapter 10

Growing Up and Getting Old

Be as understanding with your parents
as you want them to be with you.

Communicating with Our Parents

When I was growing up, my teenage years were the most difficult of all. I had so many questions, but I did not want to listen to those who thought they had the answers, especially adults. I wanted to learn everything by myself because I did not trust the information that grown-ups gave me.

I felt particular animosity towards my parents because I was an abused child. I could not understand how my stepfather could treat me the way he did, nor could I understand how my mother could simply ignore what he was doing to me. I felt cheated and misunderstood, and I was certain that my family, specifically, and the world, in general, were against me.

Through my many years spent in the counseling of others, particularly young people, I have found that many people share the same feelings about their parents that I had about mine. Some of the words I hear teenagers use

129

to describe how they feel are: *trapped*, *judged*, *watched*, and *misunderstood*.

Of course, it would be great to have parents who would be accommodating in any given situation; however, in most cases, that is not possible. Although our parents are merely human beings like the rest of us, we often feel that they are being unfair and unreasonable and have no understanding of what we are going through.

One young man I counseled had a very difficult time relating to his father. He felt that they had nothing in common, and when his father spoke to him, it was simply to utter some negative or belittling comment. I asked the young man if he knew how his grandfather had treated his father, and he admitted that he didn't. His grandfather had died before the young man was born.

I suggested that he ask his father about his own childhood and how it affected him. At first the young man was hesitant, because it was uncomfortable to talk to his father without feeling he would be ridiculed or judged. However, he took the plunge and agreed to approach his father.

The next time I saw him, the young man seemed more at ease. "Wow," he exclaimed, "I didn't realize what kind of a childhood my own father had." Apparently his grandfather had insisted that all of his children address him as *Sir*, and they lived by the old standard that children were to be seen but not heard. If they dared to utter one contrary word, they were severely beaten. No wonder his father was critical.

When we grow up, many of us have the good intentions of treating our children differently than the way we were treated. However, we learn from the world around us, and sooner or later, we begin to sound and act just like our parents.

In the case of this young man, his father inflicted the same kind of verbal abuse on his son that his own father had heaped on him. He may not have intended to do so; he was merely acting in a way consistent with his own upbringing.

However, the young man came to understand a little more about his father, and as a result, they were able to communicate more freely. Although it would take some effort and patience on both their parts before their level of communication would be ideal, at least they were both moving in a new direction.

I strongly believe that it is very important for all of us to take the time to find out more about our parents' childhoods. If your parents are still alive, you can ask them: *"What was it like when you were growing up? What was love like in your family. How did your parents punish you? What kind of peer pressure did you have to face in those days? Did your parents like the people you dated? Did you have a job while you were growing up?"*

By learning more about our parents, we can see the patterns that have shaped who they are, and, in turn, see why they treat us as they do. As we learn to empathize with our parents, we will see them in a new, more loving light. You may be able to open doors to a more communicative, loving relationship—one that has mutual respect and trust.

If you have difficulty even talking with your parents, first start in your mind or in front of the mirror. Imagine yourself telling them, "There's something I want to speak to you about." Go through this process several days in a row. It will help you decide what you want to say and how to say it.

Or, do a meditation and in your mind, talk to each of your parents and clean up your old issues. Forgive them and forgive yourself. Tell them you love them. Then, prepare to tell them the same things in person.

At one of my groups, a young man told me that he had a lot of anger and that he didn't trust others. He recycled this pattern of distrust over and over again in all his relationships. When we got to the root of the problem, he told me that he was so angry with his father for not being the person he wanted him to be.

Again, when we are on a spiritual pathway, it's not up to us to change the other person. First of all, we need to release all the pent-up feelings we harbor against our parents, and then we need to forgive them for not being who we wanted them to be. We always want everybody else to be like us, to think like us, to dress like us, to do what we do. However, as you know we are all so very different.

In order to have the space to be ourselves, we need to give that space to others. By forcing our parents to be something that they are not, we cut off our own love. We judge our parents just the way that they judge us. If we want to share with our parents, we need to begin by eradicating our own preconceived judgments of them.

Many of you continue to have power-struggle games with your parents as you grow older. Parents push a lot of buttons, so if you want to stop playing the game, you are going to have to stop taking a part in it. It is time for you to grow up and decide what you want. You can begin by calling your parents by their first names. Calling them Mommy and Daddy when you are in your 40s only keeps you stuck in the little child role. Start becoming two adults instead of parent and child.

Another suggestion is to write an affirmative treatment that details the kind of relationship you want with your mother and/or father. Begin declaring these words for yourself. After a while, you can tell him or her face to face. If your mother or father is still pushing your buttons, you are not letting either of them know how you really feel. You have a right to have the life you want. You have a right to be an adult. It may not be easy, I know. First, decide what it is that you need, and then tell your mother or father what that is. Don't make them wrong. Ask, "How can we work this out?"

Remember, with understanding comes forgiveness, and

with forgiveness comes love. When we progress to the point where we can love and forgive our parents, we will be well on our way to being able to enjoy fulfilling relationships with everyone in our lives.

Teens Need Self-Esteem

It alarms me that the rate of suicide among our teenagers is so on the rise. It seems that more and more young people feel overwhelmed by the responsibilities of life and would just as soon give up rather than to persevere and experience the multitude of adventures that life has to offer. Much of this problem has to do with the way we, as adults, expect them to respond to life situations. Do we want them to react as we would? Do we bombard them with negativity?

The period between age 10 and 15 can be a very critical time. Children in that age group have the tendency to conform, and they will do anything to be accepted by their peers. In their need for acceptance, they often hide their true feelings for fear they will not be accepted and loved for whom they really are.

The peer pressure and societal stress that I experienced when I was young pale in comparison to that which today's young people must endure, and yet, when I was 15, due to physical and mental abuse, I left school and home to be on my own. Think how jarring it must be for the child of today to have to deal with drug abuse, physical abuse, sexually transmitted dis-eases, peer pressure and gangs, family problems; and on a global level, nuclear war, environmental upheavals, crime and so much more.

As a parent, you can discuss the differences between negative and positive peer pressure with your teen. Peer pressure is all around us from the moment we are born until the day we leave the planet. We must learn how to deal with it and not let it control us.

Similarly, it is important for us to gain some knowledge and understanding of why our children are shy, mischievous, sad, slow in school, destructive, et cetera. Children are strongly influenced by the thinking, feeling patterns established in the home, and he or she makes daily choices and decisions from that belief system. If the home environment is not conducive to trusting and loving, the child will seek trust, love, and compassion elsewhere. Many gangs are a place where children feel safe. They form a family bond, no matter how dysfunctional it is.

I truly believe that a lot of hardships could be avoided if we could only get young people to ask themselves one important question before they act: *"Will this make me feel better about myself?"* We can help our teenagers see their choices in each situation. Choice and responsibility put power back into their hands. It enables them to do something without feeling like victims of the system.

If we can teach children that they are not victims and that it is possible for them to change their experiences by taking responsibility for their own lives, we will begin to see major breakthroughs.

It is vitally important to keep the lines of communication open with children, especially when they are in their teen years. Usually what happens when children start to talk about their likes and dislikes is that they are told over and over again, "Don't say that. Don't do that. Don't feel that. Don't be that way. Don't express that. Don't, don't, don't." Eventually, children stop communicating and sometimes leave home. If you want to have your children around as you grow older, keep the lines of communication open when they are younger.

Applaud your child's uniqueness. Allow your teenagers to express themselves in their own style, even if you think it's just a fad. Don't make them wrong, or tear them down. Goodness knows, I have been through many, many fads in my lifetime, and so will you and your teenagers.

Children Learn from Our Actions

Children never do what we tell them to do; they do *what* we do. We can't say, "Don't smoke," or "Don't drink," or "Don't do drugs," if *we* do them. We have to serve as examples and live the sort of life we want our children to express. When parents are willing to work on loving themselves, it's amazing to see the harmony that is achieved within the family. Children respond with a new sense of self-esteem and start to value and respect who they are.

An exercise in self-esteem that you and your children can do together is to make a list of some goals you would like to achieve. Ask your children to write down how they see themselves in ten years, in one year, in three months. What kind of lives do they want to have? What kind of friends would be most beneficial? Have them list their goals with short descriptions of each as well as how they can make their dreams come true. You do the same.

All of you might keep the lists nearby to remind yourselves of your goals. In three months' time, go over the lists together. Have the goals changed? Don't let your children beat themselves up if they didn't get as far as they wanted. They can always revise their lists. What is most important to give young people something positive to look forward to!

Separation and Divorce

If there is separation and/or divorce in the family, it is important that each parent be supportive. It's very stressful for a child to be told that the other parent is no good.

As the parent, you have to love yourself through the fears and anger to experience as much as possible. The children will pick up feelings from you. If you're going through a lot of turmoil and pain, they will surely pick that up from you. Explain to your children that your "stuff" has nothing to do with them and their inner worth.

Don't let them get the idea that anything that's happened is their fault because that is what most children think. Let them know that you love them very much and will always be there for them.

I suggest that you do mirror work with your children every morning. Do affirmations that will get you through the trying times easily and effortlessly so that everyone will be okay. Release your painful experiences with love, and affirm happiness for all concerned.

There is a wonderful group called *The California State Task Force to Promote Self-Esteem and Personal and Social Responsibility.* It was created in 1987 by Assemblyman John Vasconcellos. Among the appointed members are Jack Canfield and Dr. Emmett Miller. I support its efforts in researching and making recommendations to the government to bring self-esteem programs into schools. Other states are following suit by including self-esteem curriculum in the classroom.

I believe that we are on the brink of some major changes in our society, especially with regard to understanding our own self-worth. If teachers, especially, can get their own self-worth on the right track, they will help our children tremendously. Children reflect the social and economic pressures with which we are faced. Any program having to do with self-esteem will need to encompass students, parents, and teachers, as well as businesses and organizations.

Growing Older Graciously

So many of us fear growing old and looking old. We make growing old so terrible and unattractive. Yet, it is a normal and natural process of living. If we can't accept our inner child and be comfortable with who we were and who we are, how can we accept the next stage?

If you don't grow old, what is the alternative? You leave the planet. As a culture, we have created, what I call, "youth worship." It's all very well and good to love ourselves at certain ages, but why can't we love ourselves as we get older? We will eventually go through every age of life.

Many women feel a lot of anxiety and fear when they think about getting old. The gay community also deals with a lot of issues having to do with youth and looks and loss of beauty. Getting old may mean getting wrinkles and gray hair and saggy skin, and, yes, I want to grow old. That's all part of being here. We are on this planet to experience every part of life.

I can understand that we don't want to get old and sick, so let's separate these two ideas. Let's not imagine or envision ourselves getting sick as a way to die. I do not personally believe that we have to die with illness.

Instead, when it is our time to leave, when we have accomplished what we came here to do, we can take a nap, or go to bed at night, and leave peacefully. We don't have to become deathly ill. We don't have to be hooked to machines. We don't have to lie suffering in a nursing home in order to leave the planet. There is a tremendous amount of information available on how to stay healthy. Don't put it off, do it now. When we get older, we want to feel wonderful, so we can continue to experience new adventures.

I read something a while ago that intrigued me. It was an article about a San Francisco medical school that had discovered that the way we age is not determined by genes, but by something they call the *aging set point*—a biological time clock that exists in our minds. This mechanism actually monitors when and how we begin to age. The set point, or aging clock, is regulated in great part by one important factor: our attitudes toward growing old.

For instance, if you believe that 35 is middle aged, that belief triggers biological changes in your body that cause it to accelerate the aging process when you reach 35. Isn't it fascinating! Somewhere, somehow, we decide what is middle age and what is old age. Where are you setting that *aging set point* within you? I have this image in my mind that I am going to live to 96 years and still be active, so, it's very important that I keep myself healthy.

Remember, too, what we give out, we get back. Be aware of how you treat older people, because when you get old, that will be the way you are treated. If you believe certain concepts about old people, again, you are forming ideas that your subconscious will respond to. Our beliefs, our thoughts, our concepts about life and about ourselves, always become true for us.

Remember, I believe that you choose your parents before you were born in order to learn valuable lessons. Your Higher Self knew the experiences that were necessary for you to proceed on your spiritual course. So whatever you came to work out with your parents, get on with it. No matter what they say or do, or said or did, you are here ultimately to love yourself.

As parents, allow your children to love themselves by giving them the space to feel safe to express themselves in positive, harmless ways. Remember, too, just as we chose our parents, our children also chose us. There are important lessons for all of us to work out.

Parents who love themselves will find it easier to teach their children about self-love. When we feel good about ourselves, we can teach our children self-worth by example. The more we work on loving ourselves, the more our children will realize that it's an okay thing to do.

PART FOUR

Applying Your Inner Wisdom

*All the theories in the world are useless
unless there is action, positive change,
and finally, healing.*

Chapter 11

Receiving Prosperity

*When we get frightened, we want to
control everything, and then we shut
off the flow of our good. Trust life.
Everything we need is here for us.*

The Power within us is willing to give us our fondest
dreams and enormous plenty instantaneously. The problem is that we are not open to receiving it. If we want
something, our Higher Power doesn't say, "I'll think
about it." It readily responds, and sends it through, but
we have to be ready for it. If not, it goes back into the
storehouse of unfulfilled desires.

Many people come to my lectures and sit with their
arms folded across their bodies. I think, "How are they
going to let anything in?" It's a wonderful symbolic ges-
ture to open our arms wide so the Universe notices and
responds. For many it's very scary, because if they open
themselves up, they think they may get terrible things; and
they probably will, until they change whatever it is inside
them that believes they will attract doom and gloom.

When we use the term *prosperity*, a lot of people immediately think of money. However, there are many other concepts that come under the auspices of prosperity, such as: time, love, success, comfort, beauty, knowledge, relationships, health, and, of course, money.

If you are always feeling rushed because there isn't enough time to do everything you want, then you have lack of time. If you feel that success is beyond your reach, then you are not going to get it. If you feel life is burdensome and strenuous, then you will always feel uncomfortable. If you think you don't know very much, and you're too dumb to figure things out, you will never feel connected to the wisdom of the Universe. If you feel a lack of love and have poor relationships, then it will be difficult for you to attract love into your life.

What about beauty? There is beauty all around us. Do you experience the beauty that is abundant on the planet, or do you see everything as ugly and wasteful and dirty? How is your health? Are you sick all the time? Do you catch cold easily? Do you get many aches and pains? Finally, there is money. Many of you tell me that there is never enough money in your lives. What do you let yourself have? Or perhaps you feel you are on a fixed income. Who fixed it?

None of the above has anything to do with receiving. People always think, "Oh I want to get this and that and whatever." However, abundance and prosperity is about allowing yourself to accept. When you're not *getting* what you want, on some level you are not allowing yourself to accept. If we are stingy with life, then life will be stingy with us. If we steal from life, life will steal from us.

Being Honest With Ourselves

Honesty is a word we use a lot, not always understanding the true significance of what it means to be honest. It has nothing to do with morality or being a goodie-goodie. Being honest really has little to do with getting caught or going to jail. It is an act of love for ourselves.

The main value of honesty is that whatever we give out in life we will get back. The law of cause and effect is always operating on all levels. If we belittle or judge others, then we, too, are judged. If we are always angry, then we encounter anger wherever we go. The love we have for ourselves keeps us in tune with the love life has for us.

For instance, imagine that your apartment has just been burglarized. Do you immediately think that you are a victim? "My apartment was just ripped off! Who did this to me?" It is a devastating feeling when something like that happens; however, do you stop to think of how and why you attracted the experience?

Again, taking responsibility for creating our own experiences is not an idea that many of us want to accept all the time, perhaps just some of the time. It is so much easier to blame something outside of ourselves, yet our spiritual growth cannot occur until we recognize that there is little of value outside of us—everything comes from within.

When I hear that someone has just been robbed or experienced some kind of loss, the first question I ask is, "Whom did you steal from lately?" If a curious look comes over his or her face, I know I have touched a tender spot. When we think back to a time when we took something, and then think of what we lost shortly thereafter, the connection between the two experiences can be an eye-opener.

When we take something that isn't ours, we almost always lose something of greater value. We might take money or some object, and then we might lose a relationship. If we steal a relationship, we might lose a job. If we lift stamps and pens from the office, we might miss a train or a dinner date. The losses almost always hurt us in some important area of our lives.

It is unfortunate that many people steal from large companies, department stores, restaurants, or hotels and so on, rationalizing that these businesses can afford it. This type of rationalization does not work; the law of cause and effect continues to operate for each one of us. If we take, we lose. If we give, we get. It cannot be otherwise.

If there are many losses in your life or many things are going wrong, you might examine the ways in which you are taking. Some people, who would not dream of stealing things, will self-righteously rob another person of time or self-esteem. Each time we make another person feel guilty, we are stealing self-worth from him or her. To be truly honest on all levels takes a great deal of self-examination and self-awareness.

When we take something that does not belong to us, we are, in effect, instructing the Universe that we don't feel worthy of earning; we aren't good enough; we want to be stolen from; or there is not enough to go around. We believe that we must be sneaky and grab to get our good. These beliefs become effective walls around us that prevent us from experiencing abundance and joy in our lives.

These negative beliefs are not the truth of our being. We are magnificent and deserve the very best. This planet is abundantly plentiful. Our good always comes to us by the right of consciousness. The work we do in consciousness is always one of refining what we say and think and do. When we clearly understand that our thoughts create our reality, then we use our reality as a feedback mechanism to let us know what we need to change next. Being absolutely honest, down to the last paper clip, is a choice we make out of love for ourselves. Honesty helps to make our lives run more smoothly and more easily.

If you go to a store and they don't charge you for something you've bought and you know it, then it's your spiritual obligation to tell them so. If you are aware, you call it to their attention. If you don't know it, or only realize it when you get home or two days later, then that is something different.

If dishonesty brings disharmony into our lives, imagine what love and honesty can create. The good in our lives, the wonderful surprises we have—these, too, we have created. As we look within ourselves with honesty and unconditional love, we will discover so much about our power. What we can learn to create with our own consciousness has far greater value than any amount of money we could possibly steal.

Your Home Is Your Sanctuary

Everything is a reflection of what you believe you deserve. Look at your home. Is it a place that you really love to live in? Is it comfortable and joyous, or cramped, dirty, and always messy? The same with your car—do you like it? Does it reflect the love you have for yourself?

Are your clothes a bother and a nuisance and something you have to deal with? Your clothes are a reflection of how you feel about yourself. Again, the thoughts we have about ourselves can be changed.

If you want to find a new home, begin by opening yourself up to finding the right place, and affirm that it is waiting for you. When I was looking for a new home in Los Angeles, I couldn't believe that I would only find appalling places. I kept thinking that this is Los Angeles, and it's filled with wonderful apartments, so where are they?

It took me six months to find the one I wanted, and it was magnificent. During the time I was looking, the building was being constructed, and when it was finished, I found it waiting for me. If you look for something, but you are not finding it, there is probably a reason.

If you want to move from where you are because you don't like it, thank your present home for being there. Appreciate it for sheltering you from the weather. If it's difficult to like it, start with one part of the house that you like—it may be a corner of your bedroom. Don't say, "I hate this old place," because you are not going to find something that you love.

Love where you are, so you can be open to receiving a wonderful new home. If your home is messy and cluttered, then start cleaning it up. Your home is a reflection of who you are.

Loving Relationships

I am a great admirer of Dr. Bernie Siegel, the Connecticut oncologist, who has written, *Love, Medicine & Miracles.* Dr. Siegel has learned much from his cancer patients, and I would like to share what he says about unconditional love:

> *"Many people, especially cancer patients, grow up believing that there is some terrible flaw at the center of their being. A defect they must hide if they are to have any chance for love. Feeling unloved and unlovable and condemned to loneliness if their true selves became known. Such individuals set up defenses against sharing their innermost feelings with anyone. Because such people feel a profound emptiness inside they come to see all relationships and transactions in terms of getting something to fill the vaguely understood void within. They give love only on condition that they get something for it. And this leads to an ever deeper sense of emptiness which keeps the vicious cycle going."*

Whenever I give a lecture and allow my audience the opportunity to ask questions, I can always count on being asked one thing in particular: "How can I create healthy, lasting relationships?"

All relationships are important because they reflect how you feel about yourself. If you are constantly beating yourself up by thinking that everything that goes wrong is your fault, or that you are always a victim, then you are going to attract the type of relationships that reinforce those beliefs in you.

One woman told me that she was in a relationship with a very caring and loving man, yet she had a need to test his love. So I asked her, "Why would you test his love?" She said she felt unworthy of his love because she wasn't loving herself enough. So I suggested that three times a day she stand with her arms opened, and say, "I am willing to let the love in. It's safe to let the love in." Then I told her to look into her own eyes and say, "I deserve. I am willing to *have* even if I don't *deserve*."

Too often, you deny your good because you don't believe you can have it. For instance, you want to get married or have a long-lasting relationship. The person you go out with has four of the qualities you want in a partner. You know you're on your way. You want a little more of this or want to add something new to your list. Depending upon how much you believe you deserve to be loved, you may have to go through a dozen people before you get what you really want.

Likewise, if you believe that a Higher Power has surrounded you with truly loving people, or that everyone you meet or know brings only good into your life, then those are the types of relationships you will ultimately draw to yourself.

Codependent Relationships

Personal relationships always seem to be the first priority for many of us. Perhaps you are always searching for love. Hunting for love doesn't bring the right partner because the reasons for wanting love are unclear. We think, "Oh, if I only had someone who loved me, my life would be all better." That's not the way it works.

One exercise that I recommend is to write down the qualities you want from a relationship, such as fun, intimacy, open and positive communication, et cetera. Look at your list. Are these standards impossible to fulfill? Which of the requirements could you supply yourself?

There's a big difference between the *need for love*, and being *needy for love*. When you are *needy for love*, it simply means that you are missing love and approval from the most important person you know—yourself. You become involved in relationships that are codependent and ineffectual for both partners.

When we need someone else to fulfill us, we are codependent. When we rely on another to take care of us, so we don't have to do it ourselves, we become codependent. Many of us from dysfunctional families have learned codependency from the way we grew up. I believed for years that I was not good enough, and I sought love and approval wherever I went.

If you are always telling the other person what to do,

then you are probably trying to manipulate the relationship. On the other hand, if you are working to change your own inner patterns, then you are allowing things to happen in their right course.

Take a moment to stand in front of a mirror, and think about some of your own negative childhood beliefs that have been affecting your relationships. Can you see how you are still recreating the same beliefs? Think of some positive childhood beliefs. Do they hold the same charge for you as the negative ones?

Tell yourself that the negative beliefs no longer serve you and replace it with new, positive affirmations. You may want to write the new beliefs down and place them where you can see them every day. Again, be patient with yourself. Persevere with the new belief as much as you did with the old one. There were many times when I slipped back into old patterns before my new beliefs took root.

Remember, when you are able to contribute to the fulfillment of your own needs, then you will not be so *needy*, so codependent. It all begins with how much you love yourself. When you truly love yourself, you stay centered, calm, and secure, and your relationships at home as well as at work are wonderful. You will find yourself reacting to various situations and people differently. Matters that once may have been desperately important won't be quite as important anymore. New people will enter your life, and perhaps some old ones will disappear, which can be scary at first, and also wonderful, refreshing, and exciting.

Once you know what you want in a relationship, you must go out and be with people. No one is going to suddenly appear at your doorstep. A good way to meet people is in a support group or a night class. It enables you to connect with people who are like-minded or who are involved in the same interests. It's amazing how quickly you can meet new friends. There are many groups and classes available in cities all around the world. You need to seek these groups out. It helps when you associate with people traveling a similar path. An affirmation I suggest is: *"I am open and receptive to wonderful, good experiences coming into my life."* It's better than saying, "I'm looking for a new lover." Be open and receptive, and the Universe will respond for your highest good.

You will find that as your self-love grows, so will your self-respect, and any changes that you find yourself needing to make will be easier to accomplish when you know that they are the right ones for you. Love is never outside yourself—it is always within you. As you are more loving, you will be more lovable.

Beliefs About Money

Having fear about the issue of money comes from our early childhood programming. A woman at one of my workshops said that her wealthy father had always had a fear of going broke, and he passed on the fear that money would be taken away. She grew up being afraid that she wouldn't be taken care of. Her freedom with money was tied to the fact that her father manipulated his family through guilt. She had plenty of money all her life, and her lesson was to let go of the fear that she couldn't take care of herself. Even without all the money, she still could take care of herself.

Many of our parents grew up in the Depression, and many of us have inherited beliefs when we were young, such as, "We may starve," or "We may never find work," or "We may lose our home, our car," whatever.

Very few children say, "No that's nonsense." Children accept it and say, "Yes, that's right."

Make a list of your parents' beliefs about money. Ask yourself if you are still choosing to believe them now. You will want to go beyond your parents' limitations and fears because your life is not the same now. Stop repeating these beliefs to yourself. Begin transforming the pictures in your mind. When an opportunity comes up, don't echo your past history of lack. Begin proclaiming the new message for today. You can begin now to affirm that it's okay to have money and riches and that you will use your money wisely.

It is also normal and natural for us to have more money at certain times than others. If we can trust the Power within to always take care of us no matter what, we can easily flow through the lean times, knowing that we will have more in the future.

Money isn't the answer, although many of us think that if we have a lot of money, everything will be fine; we won't have any more problems or worries. But money is truly not the answer. Some of us have all the money that we could ever need, and we still aren't happy.

Be Grateful for What You Have

A gentleman I knew told me that he felt guilty because he couldn't pay back his friends for the kindness and gifts they gave him when he was not doing so well. I told him that there are times when the Universe gives to us, in whatever form we may need, and we may not be able to give back.

In whatever way the Universe has decided to respond to your need, be grateful. There *will* come a time when you will help somebody else. It may not be with money, but with time or compassion. Sometimes we don't realize that these things can be more valuable than money.

I can think of many people during the early days of my life who helped me enormously at a time when there was no way for me to pay them back. Years later, I have taken the opportunity to help others. Too often we feel we must exchange prosperity. We must reciprocate. If somebody takes us to lunch, we immediately have to take them to lunch; or somebody gives us a gift, and we immediately have to buy one for them.

Learn to receive with thanks. Learn to accept because the Universe perceives our openness to receive as not just exchanging prosperity. Much of our problem stems from our in-ability to receive. We can give but it's so difficult to receive.

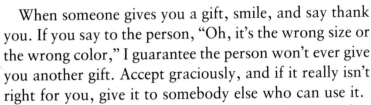

When someone gives you a gift, smile, and say thank you. If you say to the person, "Oh, it's the wrong size or the wrong color," I guarantee the person won't ever give you another gift. Accept graciously, and if it really isn't right for you, give it to somebody else who can use it.

We want to be grateful for what we do have, so that we can attract more good to us. Again, if we focus on lack, then we will draw it to us. If we are in debt, we need to forgive ourselves, not berate ourselves. We need to focus on the debt being paid off by doing affirmations and visualizations.

The best thing we can do for people who are having money problems is to teach them how to create it in consciousness, because then it's lasting. It's much more lasting than handing them some money. I'm not saying, don't give your money away, but don't give it away because you feel guilty. People seem to say, "Well I have to help other people." You're a *people*, too. You are somebody, and you're worthy of prosperity. Your consciousness is the best bank account you can have. When you put in worthwhile thoughts, you will reap large dividends.

Tithing Is a Universal Principle

One of the ways to attract money into your life is to tithe. Tithing 10% of you income has long been an established principle. I like to think of it as *giving back to Life*. When we do that we seem to prosper more. The churches have always wanted you to tithe to them. It is one of their principle ways of gathering income. In current years that has expanded to tithing to where you get your spiritual food.

Who or what has nourished you on your quest for improving the quality of your life? That could be the perfect place for you to tithe. If tithing to a church or a person doesn't appeal to you, there are many wonderful non-profit organizations that could benefit others by your contributions. Investigate and find the one that is right for you.

People often say, "I will tithe when I have more money." Of course then they never do. If you are going to tithe, start now and watch the blessings flow. However if you only tithe to *get more,* then you have missed the point. It must be freely given or it won't work. I feel that life has been good to me and I gladly give to life in various ways.

There is so much abundance in this world just waiting for you to experience it. If you would know that there is more money than you could ever spend, or more people than you could ever meet, and more joy than you could imagine, you would have everything you need and desire.

If you ask for your highest good, then trust the Power within to provide it to you. Be honest with yourself and others. Don't cheat, not even a little, it will only come back to you.

The Infinite Intelligence that permeates all says "Yes!" to you. When something comes into your life, don't push it away, say "Yes!" to it. Open yourself to receiving good. Say "Yes!" to your world. Opportunity and prosperity will increase a hundredfold.

Chapter 12

Expressing Your Creativity

When our inner vision opens, our horizons expand.

Our Work Is a Divine Expression

When people ask me about my purpose in life, I tell them that my work is my purpose. It is very sad to know that most people hate their jobs and even worse, that they don't know what they want to do. Finding your life's purpose, finding work that you love to do, is loving who you are.

Your work serves as your expression of creativity. You need to go beyond your feelings of not being good enough or not knowing enough. Allow the creative energy of the Universe to flow through you in ways that are deeply satisfying to you. It doesn't matter what you do, as long as it is satisfying to your being and it fulfills you.

If you hate where you work or hate what you're doing, you will always feel the same about your job unless you change inside. If you go to a new job with your same old work beliefs, you will only feel the same way again in time.

161

Part of the problem is that many people ask for what they want in a negative way. One woman had a very difficult time stating what she wanted in a positive way. She kept repeating, "I don't want this to be a part of the job," or "I don't want this to happen," or "I don't want to feel the negative energy there." Can you see that she was not declaring what she did want? We need to be clear on what we want!

Sometimes it's troublesome to ask for what we want. It's so easy to say what we don't want. Start declaring what you want your work to be. *"My work is deeply fulfilling. I help people. I am able to be aware of what they need. I work with people that love me. I feel safe at all times."* Or perhaps, *"My work allows me to express my creativity freely. I earn good money doing things I love."* Or, *"I am always happy at work. My career is filled with joy and laughter and abundance."*

Always declare in the present tense. What you declare, you will get! If you don't, then there are beliefs within you that are refusing to accept your good. Make a list of *What I believe about work.* You may be amazed at the negative beliefs within you. You won't prosper until you change those beliefs.

When you work at a job you hate, you are shutting down the ability of your Power to express itself. Think of the qualities you want in a job—what it would feel like if you had the perfect job. It is essential that you are clear about what you do want. Your Higher Self will find a job that is right for you. If you don't know, be willing to know. Open yourself to the wisdom that is inside you.

I learned early through Science of Mind that my job was to express Life. Every time I was presented with a problem, I knew it was an opportunity to grow and that the Power that created me had given me everything I needed to solve that problem. After my initial panic, I would quiet my mind and turn within. I gave thanks for the opportunity to demonstrate the Power of the Divine Intelligence working through me.

A woman at one of my workshops wanted to be an actress. Her parents persuaded her to attend law school, and she was under a lot of pressure from everyone around her to go into law. However, she stopped going after one month. She decided to take an acting class because that is what she always wanted to do.

Soon after, she started having dreams that she was going nowhere in her life, and she became miserable and depressed. She was having a problem letting go of her doubts and had reservations about making the biggest mistake in her life, which she feared she could never go back and change.

I asked her, "Whose voice is that in there?" She said those were the words that her father had told her several times.

There are many people who can relate to this young woman's story. She wanted to act, and her parents wanted her to be a lawyer. She got to a point of confusion, not knowing what to do. She needed to understand that it was her father's way of saying, "I love you." If she became a lawyer, he felt she would be safe and secure. That's what he wanted. However, it's not what *she* wanted.

She had to do what was right for her life even if it did not meet her fathers' expectations. I told her to sit in front of the mirror and look into her eyes and say, *"I love you, and I support you in having what you really want. I'm going to support you in every way that I can."*

I told her to take the time to listen. She needed to connect to her inner wisdom and realize that she didn't have to please anyone other than herself. She could love her father and still fulfill herself. She had the right to feel worthy and able to do it. And she could tell her father, "I love you and I don't want to be a lawyer—I want to be an actress," or whatever. It is one of our challenges to do what is right for us even when those who care about us have other ideas. We are not here to fulfill other peoples expectations.

When we have strong beliefs that we don't deserve, we have problems doing what we want. If other people tell you that you can't have, and then you deny yourself, the child inside you doesn't believe it deserves anything good. Again, it comes back to learning and practicing ways to love yourself more each day.

I repeat, do begin by writing down everything you believe about work and failure and success. Look at all the negatives, and realize that those are the beliefs that keep you from flowing in this area. You may find you have many beliefs that say you deserve to fail. Take each negative statement and turn it into a positive one. Begin to shape in your mind what you want your fulfilling work to be.

Your Income Can Come from Many Sources

How many of us believe that we have to work hard to earn a good living? Especially in this country, there is a work ethic that implies that one must work hard to be a good person, and in addition to that, work is drudgery.

I have found that if you work at what you love, you can usually create a good income for yourself. If you continually say, "I hate this job," you will get nowhere. Whatever you are doing, bring love and a positive attitude into it. If you are in an uncomfortable situation, look within to see what is the best lesson for you to learn from it.

One young woman told me that her belief system allowed money to come to her from all sorts of unexpected sources. Her friends criticized her ability to draw wealth to her in her unique way and insisted that she had to work hard to earn money. She said that they knew she didn't work hard at all. So she began to run the fear that if she didn't work hard, that meant that she didn't deserve the money she had.

Her consciousness was on the right track originally. She needed to thank herself instead of becoming fearful. She understood how to manifest abundance, and her life was working in that area without any struggle. However, her friends wanted to pull her down because they all worked hard and they didn't have as much money as she did.

Many times I reach out my hand to others, and if they take it and want to learn new things and go places, it's wonderful. If they try and drag me down, I say goodbye, and I work with somebody who really wants to come up out of the mud.

If your life is filled with love and joy, don't listen to some miserable, lonely person who tells you how to run your life. If your life is rich and abundant, don't listen to someone who is poor and in debt tell you how to run it. Very often, our parents are the ones telling us how to do things. They come from a place of burden and hardship and misery and then try to tell us how to run our lives!

Many people worry about the economy and believe they will either earn or lose money due to the economic situation at present. However, the economy is always moving up and down. So, it doesn't matter what is happening out there, or what others do to change the economy. We are not stuck because of the economy. No matter what is happening "out there" in the world, it only matters what you believe about yourself.

If you have a fear about becoming homeless, ask yourself, "Where am I not at home within my self? Where do I feel abandoned? What do I need to do to experience inner peace?" All outer experiences reflect inner beliefs. I have always used the affirmation, *"My income is constantly increasing."* Another affirmation I like is, *"I go beyond my parents' income level.* You have a right to earn more than your parents' did. It's almost a necessity since things cost more now. Women, especially, experience a lot of conflict with this one. Often they find it difficult to earn more than their fathers are earning. They need to go beyond their feelings of not deserving and accept the abundance of financial wealth that is their divine right.

Your job is only one of many channels of an infinite source of money. Money is not the object of your right work. Money can come to you in many ways and from many avenues. No matter how it comes, accept it with joy as a gift from the ~~Universe~~. God

A young lady was complaining that her in-laws were buying her new baby all sorts of nice things and she could not afford to buy anything. I reminded her that the ~~Universe~~ wanted that baby to be well supplied with an abundance of all good and used the in-laws as a channel to supply it. She then could be grateful and appreciate the way in which the ~~Universe~~ was providing for her baby.

Relationships on the Job

The relationships we create at work are similar to the relationships we have as a family. They can be healthy or they can be dysfunctional.

A woman once asked me, "As a person who is usually positive, how do I deal with people in a work environment who are constantly negative?"

First of all, I thought it interesting that she was in a

work environment where everybody was negative when she said she was positive. I wondered why she was attracting negativity to her, perhaps there was negativity within her that she did not recognize.

I suggested that she start to believe for herself that she always worked in an area where it was peaceful and joyful, where people really appreciated each other and life as a whole. Where there was respect on all sides. Instead of complaining how so-and-so had to do it his way, she could affirm for herself that she always worked in the ideal place.

By adopting this philosophy she could either help bring out the best qualities in others because they would be responding differently to her inner changes, or she would find herself in another work arena where the conditions would be as she declared.

A man once told me that when he started his job he had all these incredible instincts, and his job was wonderful and sailed along smoothly. He was precise, direct, and satisfied. Suddenly, he began to make mistakes every day. I asked him what he was frightened of? Could it be an old childhood fear that was surfacing? Was there someone at work with whom he was angry, or was he trying to get even with somebody? Did that person remind him of one of his parents? Had this happened in other jobs? It seemed to me that he was creating some chaos at work because of an old belief system. He recognized that it was an old family pattern where he was ridiculed every time he made a mistake. I suggested that he forgive his family and affirm that he now has wonderful, harmonious relationships at work where people totally respect him and appreciate everything he does.

When you think of your co-workers, don't think, "They're so negative." Everybody has every quality in them, so respond to the good qualities that are in them, and respect their peacefulness instead. When you can focus on these qualities, they will rise to the surface. If others are constantly saying negative things, don't pay attention. You want to change *your* consciousness. Since they are reflecting something negative within you, when your consciousness really changes, negative people won't be around very much. Even if you feel frustrated, start affirming what you want to have in your work space. Then accept it with joy and thanksgiving.

One woman had an opportunity at work to do what she loved and to grow from the experience. However, she would constantly get sick and sabotage herself. She recalled that when she was a child she was always getting sick because it was her way of getting love and affection. So she kept recreating the pattern of getting sick as an adult.

What she needed to learn was how to get love and affection in a more positive way. When anything went wrong at work, she went right back to being the five-year-old girl. So when she began to take care of her little inner child she also learned to feel safe, and to accept her own power.

Competition and comparison are two major stumbling blocks to your creativity. Your uniqueness sets you apart from all others. There has never been another person like you since time began, so what is there to compare or compete with? Comparison either makes you feel superior or inferior, which are expressions of your ego, your limited-mind thinking. If you are going to compare to make yourself feel a little bit better, then you are saying somebody else isn't good enough. If you put others down, you may think you will raise yourself up. What you really do is put yourself in a position to be criticized by others. We all do this on some level and its good when we can transcend it. Becoming enlightened is to go within and shine the light on yourself so you can dissolve whatever darkness that is in there.

I want to say, again, that everything changes, and what was perfect for you once, may not be anymore. In order for you to keep changing and growing, you keep going within and listening for that which is right for you in the here and now.

Changing the Way We Do Business

For the past several years, I have owned my own publishing business. My motto has been that we open the mail and answer the phone, and handle what's in front of us, and there is always plenty to do. As we did this day by day, the business grew from a few people to well over 20 employees.

We established our business on spiritual principles, using affirmative mind treatments to open and close meetings. We realized that many other businesses ran on competition, often condemning others, and we did not want to put that energy out to others, knowing that it would come back two-fold.

We decided that if we were going to live by the philosophy, we were not going to operate under the old concepts of doing business. If problems arose, we would spend time affirming what we wanted to change.

We also had a soundproof *"screaming room,"* where employees could let off steam without being heard or judged. It was also a place where they could meditate or relax, and we supplied it with plenty of tapes for people to listen to. It became a safe haven in times of difficulty.

I remember a time when we were having many problems with our computer system, and every day something would break down. Because I believe machines reflect our consciousness, I realized that many of us were sending negative energy to the computers and we were *expecting* them to constantly break down. I had an affirmation programmed into the computer, "Good Morning, how are you today? I work well when I am loved. I love you." In the morning when everyone turned on their computers, that message would appear. Its amazing how we had no more problems with our computers.

Sometimes we think of things that happen, especially at work, as "disasters." But we must look at them for what they are—simply life experiences that *always* teach us something. I know that I have never had a "disaster" that did not end up a good learning experience in the end, and it often moved me to a much better level in life.

For instance, recently my company, Hay House, was not doing so well. Like the economy, our sales would go up and down and it appeared that sales were down and staying that way, at least for the moment. However, we did not adjust to that and month after month we were spending more than we took in. Anyone who has owned a business knows that that is not the way to do it. Eventually it looked as if I would lose my business if I didn't take some "drastic measures."

Those "drastic measures" included letting go of over half of my staff. You can imagine how difficult it was for me to do that. I remember walking into the conference room, where all my staff had gathered, to deliver the news. I was in tears, but I knew that it had to be done. As difficult as it was for all of us, I also trusted that my much loved employees would soon find new and better jobs. And almost all of them have! Some of them have even started their own businesses and are very successful. At the darkest time I kept knowing and affirming that this experience would turn out to be for the highest good of all concerned.

Of course, everyone else assumed the worst. Rumors were flying that Hay House was belly up. Not just within the people I knew, but all over the country! Our sales staff were surprised that so many business people even *knew* about our company, let alone its financial condition. I have to admit that we took great joy in proving those forecasts wrong. By tightening our belts tremendously, we didn't go belly up. With our smaller staff, and each of us determined to make it work, we've come through it very well, but most importantly *we have learned a lot.*

In the meantime, Hay House is now doing better than ever. My staff is enjoying their work and I am enjoying my staff. Even though we are all working harder, the interesting thing is that no one feels that they have too much work to do. We are even getting more books out than we ever had and are attracting much more prosperity in all areas of our lives.

I believe that everything does work out for the best in the end, but sometimes it is hard to see that while you are going through the experience. Think of a negative experience that may have happened to you in your work or in you past, in general. Perhaps you were fired or maybe your spouse left you. Now go beyond it and take a look at the big picture. Didn't many good things happen as a result of that experience? I've heard so many times, "Yes, that was a horrible thing that happened to me, but if it hadn't, I never would have met so-and-so . . . or start my own business . . . or admit that I had an addiction . . . or learn to love myself."

By trusting the Divine Intelligence to let us experience life in the way that is best for us, we empower ourselves to actually enjoy *everything* that life has to offer; the good as well as the so-called bad. Try applying this to your work experiences and notice the changes that happen to you.

Those who own or operate businesses can begin to function as an expression of Divine Intelligence. It is important to keep the lines of communication open with employees and allow them to express their feelings about their work in a safe way. Make sure the offices are a neat and clean place to work. Here again, clutter in an office reflects the consciousness of the people working there. With all the physical clutter, how can the mental or intellectual tasks be done well and on time? You could adopt a statement of purpose that reflects the desired philosophy of your business. At Hay House we feel our purpose is: "*Creating a world where it is safe for us to love each other.*" When you allow Divine Intelligence to operate in all aspects of business, then everything flows on purpose and according to a divine plan. The most wonderful opportunities will fall in your lap.

I see many businesses beginning to change. There will come a time when business will not be able to survive using the old ways of competition and conflict. One day we will all know that there is plenty for everyone and that we bless and prosper each other. Companies can begin to shift their priorities and make it a great place for their workers to express themselves, and have their products and services benefit the planet in general.

People want to get more out of their work than just a paycheck. They want to contribute to the world and feel fulfilled. In the future, the ability to do good on a global level will overshadow the need for materialism.

Chapter 13

The Totality of Possibilities

Each one of us is totally linked with the Universe and with all of life. The Power is within us to expand the horizons of our consciousness.

Now I want you to stretch even further. If you have been on the pathway and doing work on yourself for some time, does that mean you have nothing else to do? Are you really going to sit on your laurels and rest? Or do you realize that this inner work is a lifetime occupation, and once you start, you really never stop? You can hit plateaus and take vacations, but basically it's a lifetime's worth of work. You may want to ask yourself what areas you still need to work on and what you need. Are you healthy? Are you happy? Are you prosperous? Are you creatively fulfilled? Do you feel safe? Do you feel secure?

Limitations Learned from the Past

There is an expression I like to use a lot—*the totality of possibilities*. I learned it from one of my early teachers in

175

New York—Eric Pace. It always gave me such a taking-off place for letting my mind go beyond what I thought possible; far beyond the limited beliefs I grew up with when I was young.

Being a child, I didn't understand that the passing criticisms of grown-ups and friends were just the result of a bad day or a small disappointment and really weren't true. I accepted these thoughts and beliefs about myself willingly, and they became a part of my limitations. I may not have looked awkward, or dumb, or silly, but I sure felt it.

Most of us create the ideas we believe about life by the time we are five years old. We add a little bit more when we are teenagers, and maybe a tiny bit more when we're older, but very little. If I were to ask most people why they believe such and such on any subject, and they trace it back, they would discover that they made a certain decision about the subject by the time they were this young age.

So, we live in the limitations of our five-year-old consciousness. It was something we accepted from our parents, and we still live under the limitations of our parents' consciousness. Even the most wonderful parents in the world didn't know everything and had their own limitations. We say what they said and do what they did: "You can't do that," or "That won't work." However, we don't need limitations, as important as they may seem.

Some of our beliefs may be positive and nourishing. These thoughts served us well all of our lives, such as, "Look both ways before you cross the street," or "Fresh fruits and vegetables are good for your body." Other thoughts may be useful at a young age, but as we grow older, they are no longer appropriate. "Don't trust strangers," for instance, may be good advice for a small child. As adults, to perpetuate this belief only creates isolation and loneliness. The good news in all of this is that we can always make adjustments all the time.

The moment we say "I can't," or "It won't work," or "There's not enough money,"or "What would the neighbors think?" we are limited. This last expression is a significant obstacle for us. "What will the neighbors, or my friends, or my co-workers, or whoever, think?" It's a good excuse—now we don't have to do it, because *they* wouldn't do it, and *they* wouldn't approve. As society changes, what the neighbors think changes, also, so to hold on to this assumption doesn't make sense.

If someone says to you, "Nobody has ever done it this way before," you can say, "So what?" There are hundreds of ways of doing something, so do the way that's right for you. We tell ourselves other absurd messages such as, "I'm not strong enough," or I'm not young enough," or "I'm not old enough," or I'm not tall enough, or "I'm not the right sex."

How often have you used the last one? "Because I'm a woman, I can't do this," or "Because I'm a man, I can't do that." Your soul has no sexuality. I believe you agreed upon your sexuality before you were born to learn a spiritual lesson. To feel inferior because of sexuality is not only a poor excuse but also another way to relinquish your power.

Our limitations often stop us from expressing and experiencing the totality of possibilities. "I don't have the right education." How many of us have let that one stop us? We have to realize that education is something set up by groups of people who say, "You can't do such and such unless you do it our way." We can accept that as a limitation, or we can go beyond it. I accepted it for many, many years because I was a high school drop-out. I used to say, "Oh, I don't have any education. I can't think. I can't get a good job. I can't do anything well."

Then one day I realized that the limitation was all in my mind and had nothing to do with reality. When I dropped my own limiting beliefs, and I allowed myself to move into the totality of possibilities, I discovered that I could think. I discovered that I was very bright, and I could communicate. I discovered all sorts of possibilities, which when viewed from the limitations of the past seemed impossible.

Limiting the Potential Within Us

Then, there are some of you who think you know it all. The trouble with knowing it all is that you don't grow, and nothing new can come in. Do you accept that there is a Power and an Intelligence greater than you, or do you think that you are "it"—you in your physical body? If you think that you're "it," then you will be running scared because of your limited mind. If you realize that there is a Power in this Universe that is far greater and wiser, and you are a part of It, then you can move into the space where the totality of possibilities can operate.

How often do you allow yourself to dwell in the limitations of your present consciousness? Every time you say, "I can't," you are putting a stop sign in front of you. You shut down the door to your own inner wisdom, and you block the flow of energy that is your spiritual knowingness. Are you willing to go beyond what you believe today? You woke up this morning with certain concepts and ideas. You have the ability to move beyond some of them to experience a far greater reality. It is called learning—because you are taking in something new. It may fit in with what is already there, or it may even be better.

Have you ever noticed that when you start rearranging your closet, you discard clothes and odds and ends that you no longer need. You pile up the possessions you are giving away on one side, and throw away the stuff that is no longer usable. Then you begin to put everything back, and in a totally different order. It's easier to find what you're looking for, and at the same time, you made room for new clothes. If you bought a new outfit and put it in the old closet, you may have had to jam it between other paraphernalia. If you clean out your closet and rearrange it, then when you bring in the new outfit, it has room for itself.

We need to do the same routine with our minds. We need to clean out the contents that no longer work so we have room for the new possibilities. Where God is, all things are possible, and God is in each one of us. If we continue with our preconceived ideas, then we are blocked. When someone is ill, do you say, "Oh, poor person, how he or she must be suffering!" Or, do you look at the person and see the absolute truth of being and affirm the health of the Divine Power that is within? Do you see the totality of possibilities and know that miracles can happen?

A man I once met told me very emphatically that it was absolutely impossible for a grown person to change. He was living in the desert and had all sorts of illnesses, and he wanted to sell his property. He didn't want to change his thinking, so he was very rigid when it came time to negotiate with a buyer. It had to be done his way. It was apparent that he would have a very burdensome time trying to sell his property because his belief was that he could never change. All he had to do was open his consciousness to a new way of thinking.

Expanding Our Horizons

How do we keep ourselves from moving into this totality of possibilities? What else limits us? All our fears are limitations. If you are frightened and you say, "I can't; it won't work," what will happen? Fearful experiences will come back. Judgments are limitations. None of us like to be judged, yet how often do we do it? We're encouraging limitations by our judgments. Every time you find yourself judging or criticizing, no matter how small, remind yourself that what goes out comes back. You may want to stop limiting your possibilities and change your thinking to something wonderful.

There is a difference between being judgmental and having an opinion. Many of you are asked for your judgment of something. In actuality, you are really giving your opinion. An opinion is how you feel about something, such as, "I prefer not to do this. I prefer to wear red instead of blue." To say someone else is wrong because she wears blue becomes a judgment. We need to discern between the two. Remember, criticism is always making yourself or someone else wrong. If someone asks your opinion, your preference, don't let it become a judgment or criticism against something else.

Similarly, every time you indulge in guilt, you are setting a limitation. If you hurt someone, say you're sorry, and don't hurt the person anymore. Don't walk around feeling guilty because it keeps you locked out from experiencing your good and has nothing to do with the reality of your true being.

When you are unwilling to forgive, you limit your growth. Forgiveness allows you to right a wrong in your spiritual self, to have understanding instead of resentment, to have compassion instead of hatred.

Look at your problems as opportunities for you to grow. When you have problems, do you see only the restrictions of your limited-mind thinking? Do you think, "Oh, poor me, why did it happen to me?" You don't always have to know how situations are going to work out. You need to trust the Power and Presence within, which is far greater than you are. You need to affirm that all is well and everything is working out for your highest good. If you open yourself to the possibilities when you have problems, you can make changes; changes can happen in incredible ways, perhaps ways you could not even imagine.

We've all been in situations in our lives where we've

said, "I don't know how I'll work this out." It seemed like we were up against a brick wall, and yet we are all here now, and we've worked through whatever it was. Maybe we didn't understand how it happened, yet it did happen. The more we can align ourselves with the cosmic energy, the One Intelligence, the Truth and Power within us, the quicker those wonderful possibilities can be realized.

Group Consciousness

It is essential that we leave our limited thinking and beliefs behind and awaken our consciousness to a more cosmic view of life. The development of higher consciousness on this planet is happening at a rate far faster than ever before. The other day I saw a graph that just fascinated me. It showed the growth of various systems in our history and how they have changed. Agricultural development was overshadowed by industrial growth, and then around 1950, the informational phase took over as communication and computer operation became widespread.

Alongside this informational period, there is also a consciousness-raising movement graph that is shooting far ahead of the informational phase at a unchallenged rate of advancement. Can you imagine what it means? I do a lot of traveling, and wherever I go, I see people who are studying and learning. I've been to Australia, Jerusalem, London, Paris, and Amsterdam, and everywhere I go I meet large groups of people who are searching for ways to expand and enlighten themselves. They are fascinated by how their minds work, and they are using their wisdom to take control of their lives and their experiences.

We are reaching new levels of spirituality. Although religious wars are still being fought, they are becoming less and less prevalent. We are beginning to connect with one another on higher levels of consciousness. The collapse of the Berlin wall and the birth of freedom in Europe are examples of our expanding consciousness, as freedom is our natural birthright. As the consciousness of each person awakens, group consciousness becomes influenced as well.

Every time you use your consciousness in a positive way, you are connecting with other people who are doing the same. Every time you use it in a negative way, you are also connecting to that. Every time you meditate, you are connecting with other people on the planet who are meditating. Every time you visualize good for yourself, you do it for others as well. Every time you visualize the healing of your body, you connect with others who are doing the same thing.

Our goals are to expand our thinking and to go beyond what was, to what might be. Our consciousness can create miracles in the world.

The totality of possibilities connects everything, including our Universe and beyond. What are you connecting with? Prejudice is a form of fear. If you're prejudiced, you are connecting with other prejudiced people. If you open your consciousness and do the best you can to work on a level of unconditional love, then you connect with the curve on the graph that is climbing upwards. Do you want to be left behind? Or do you want to go up with the curve?

Often there is a crisis in the world. How many people send positive energy to the troubled area and do affirmations that everything works out as quickly as possible and that there is a solution for the highest good of all concerned? You need to use your consciousness in a way that will create harmony and plenty for all people. What sort of energy are you sending? Instead of condemning and complaining, you can connect with the Power on the spiritual level and affirm the most positive results imaginable.

How far are you willing to expand the horizons of your thinking? Are you willing to go beyond your neighbors'? If your neighbors are limited, make new friends. How far will you stretch? How willing are you to change *I can't* to *I can.*

Every time you hear that something is incurable, know in your mind that it isn't true. Know that there is a Power greater. "Incurable" to me means that the medical profession simply hasn't yet figured out how to cure that particular illness. It doesn't mean that it's not possible. It means that we go within and find a cure. We can go beyond statistics. We are not numbers on a chart. Those are someone else's projections, somebody's limited-mind thinking. If we don't give ourselves possibilities, we don't give ourselves hope. Dr. Donald M. Pachuta at the National Aids Conference in Washington, D.C., said that "we have never had an epidemic—*ever*—that was 100 percent fatal."

Somewhere on this planet, someone has been healed of every single dis-ease that we have been able to create. If we just accept doom and gloom, we are stuck. We need to take a positive approach so we can find some answers. We need to begin to use the Power within us to heal ourselves.

Our Other Powers

It is said that we use only 10 percent of our brain—only 10 percent! What is the purpose of the other 90 percent? I think having psychic ability, telepathy, clairvoyance, or clairaudience are all normal and natural. It's just that we don't allow ourselves to experience these phenomena. We have all sorts of reasons why we don't, or why we don't believe we can. Little children are often very psychic. Unfortunately, parents immediately say, "Don't say that," or "That's your imagination," or "Don't believe in that foolish nonsense." The child inevitably turns off these abilities.

I think the mind is capable of remarkable things, and I know for certain that I could go from New York to Los Angeles without a plane if I only knew how to dematerialize and rematerialize there. I don't know how yet, but I know it is possible.

I think that we are capable of accomplishing incredible achievements, but we haven't the knowledge yet because we won't use it for our good. We will probably hurt others with the knowledge. We have to get to a point where we really can live in unconditional love, so we can begin using the other 90 percent of our brains.

Fire Walking

How many have heard about fire walking? Whenever I ask this question at seminars, several hands always go up. We all know that it is totally impossible to walk on hot coals, right? Nobody can do it without burning their feet. Yet people have done it, and they aren't extraordinary people; they are people like you and me. They probably learned it in one evening by attending a fire-walking workshop.

I have a friend, Darby Long, who works with Dr. Carl Simonton, the cancer specialist. They do a week-long workshop for people with cancer, and during the week, they have a fire-walking demonstration. Darby has done it herself many times, and has even carried people across the hot coals. I always think how incredible it must be for people with cancer to see and experience such a process. It probably blows a lot of people's minds. Their concepts about limitation would somehow be different afterward.

I believe Anthony Robbins, the young man who started fire walking in this country, is here to do something really extraordinary on the planet. He studied NLP, Neuro-linguistic Programming, a process whereby he could observe someone's patterns of behavior and then repeat that person's responses and cues of behavior to achieve similar results. NLP is based on the hypnotic techniques of Milton Erickson, M.D. which were systematically observed and recorded by John Grinder and Richard Bandler. When Tony heard about fire walking, he wanted to learn it, and, in turn, to teach it to others. He was told by a yogi that it would take years of study and meditation. However, using NLP, Tony learned it within a few hours. He knew that if he could do it, anyone could do it. He has been teaching people how to walk on coals, not because it is a wonderful parlor trick, but because it shows them how to go beyond their limitations and fears.

Everything Is Possible

Repeat with me: *"I live and dwell in the totality of possibilities. Where I am there is all good."* Think about these words for a minute. *All good.* Not some, not a little bit, but *all good.* When you believe that anything is possible, you open yourself up to answers in every area of your life.

Where we are is the totality of possibilities. It is always up to us individually and collectively. We either have walls around us or we take them down and feel safe enough to be totally open to allow all good to come into our lives. Begin to observe yourself objectively. Notice what is going on inside you—how you feel, how you react, what you believe—and allow yourself to observe without comment or judgment. When you can, you will live your life from the totality of possibilities.

PART FIVE

Letting Go of the Past

The planet is becoming conscious as a whole. It is becoming self-conscious.

Chapter 14

Change and Transition

*Some people would rather leave the
planet than change.*

Change is usually what we want the other person to do,
isn't it? When I speak about the other person, I want to
include the government, big business, the boss or co-
worker, the Internal Revenue Service, foreigners; the
school, husband, wife, mother, father, children, et cetera
—anyone other than ourselves. We don't want to change,
but we want everybody else to change so our lives will be
different. And yet, of course, any changes that we are going to make at all have to come from within ourselves.

Change means that we free ourselves from feelings of
isolation, separation, loneliness, anger, fear and pain. We
create lives filled with wonderful peacefulness, where we
can relax and enjoy life as it comes to us—where we
know that everything will be all right. I like to use the
premise that *"Life is wonderful, all is perfect in my world,
and I always move into greater good."* In that way, it
doesn't matter to me which direction my life takes, because I know it's going to be wonderful. Therefore, I can
enjoy all sorts of situations and circumstances.

191

Someone at one of my lectures was going through a lot of turmoil, and the word *pain* kept coming up in the conversation. She asked if there was another word that she could use. I thought about the time I had smashed my finger by slamming a window on it. I knew if I gave into the pain, I was going to go through a very difficult period. So when it happened, I started to do some mental work right away and referred to my finger as having a lot of *sensation*. By viewing what happened in that particular way, I think it helped to heal the finger much more quickly and to handle what could have been a very unpleasant experience. Sometimes if we can alter our thinking a little bit, we can completely change a situation.

Can you think of change as an internal housecleaning? If you do a little bit at a time, it will eventually all get done. You don't have to do it all, however, before you begin to see results. If you change just a little bit, you'll begin to feel better soon.

I was at the Reverend O.C. Smith's City of Angels Science of Mind Church on New Year's Day, and he said something that made me think. He said:

"It's the new year, but you've got to realize that the new year is not going to change you. Just because it's a new year, it's not going to make any difference in your life. The only way there's going to be a change is if you are willing to go within and make the change."

That's so true. People make all sorts of New Year's resolutions, but because they don't make any internal changes, the resolutions fall away very quickly. "I'm not going to smoke another cigarette," or whatever, someone says. Right away, it's put in a negative phrase rather than one that will tell the subconscious mind what to do. In this situation you could say instead, "All desire for cigarettes has left me and I am free."

Until we make the inner changes, until we are willing to do the mental work, nothing outside of us is going to change. Yet, the inner changes can be so incredibly simple because the only thing we really need to change are our thoughts. *Stinken Thinken*

What can you do for yourself this year that you didn't do last year that could be positive? Take a moment and think about this question. What would you like to let go of this year that you clung to so tightly last year? What would you like to change in your life? Are you willing to do it?

There is a lot of information available that will give you ideas once you are willing to change. The moment you are willing to change, it is remarkable how the Universe *God* begins to help you. It brings you what you need. It could be a book, a tape, a teacher or even a friend making a passing remark that suddenly has deep meaning to you.

Sometimes conditions will get worse before they get better, and that's okay because the process is beginning. The old threads are untangling, so flow with it. Don't panic and think its not working. Just keep working with your affirmations and the new beliefs you are planting.

Making Progress

Of course, from the moment you decide to make a change until you get the demonstration, there is a transitional period. You vacillate between the old and the new. You go back and forth between what was and what you would like to be or to have. It is a normal and natural process. Often I hear people saying, "Well, I know all this stuff." My answer is, "Are you doing it?" Knowing what to do and doing it are two separate steps. It takes time until you are strong in the new and have gone the complete shift. Until then, you must be vigilant in your efforts to change.

For instance, many people say their affirmations maybe three times and give up. Then they say that affirmations don't work, or they're silly, or whatever. We have to give ourselves time to practice to make the changes; change requires action. As I said, it's what you do after you say your affirmations that counts the most.

As you go through this transitional phase, remember to praise yourself for each small step forward that you make. If you beat yourself up for the step backward, then change becomes oppressive. Use all the tools available to you as you move from the old to the new. Assure the little child inside that he or she is safe.

Author Gerald Jampolsky says that love is letting go of fear, and that there is either fear or there is love. If we are not coming from the loving space of the heart, then we're in fear, and all those states such as isolation, separation, anger, guilt, and loneliness are part of the fear syndrome. We want to move from fear into love and make love a more permanent position for us.

There are a variety of ways to change. What do you do on a daily basis to make yourself feel good inside? You're not going to do it by blaming other people or by being a victim. So what is it you do? How are you experiencing peace within you and around you? If you are not doing it now, are you willing to begin? Are you willing to start creating inner harmony and peace?

Another question to ask yourself is: Do I really want to change? Do you want to continue to complain about what you don't have in your life? Do you want to really create a much more wonderful life than you have now? If you are willing to change, you can. If you are willing to do the work involved, then you can change your life for the better. I have no power over you, and I can't do it for you. You have the power and you need to keep reminding yourself of that.

Remember, maintaining inner peace will help us connect with like-minded, peaceful people all over the world. Spirituality connects us all over this planet on a soul level, and the sense of cosmic spirituality that we are just beginning to experience is going to change the world for the better.

When I speak of spirituality, I don't necessarily mean

religion. Religions tell us who to love and how to love and who is worthy. To me we are all worthy of love, and we are all lovable. Our spirituality is our direct connection with ~~our higher source~~, and we don't need a middleman for that. Begin to see that spirituality can connect us all over the planet on a very deep soul level.

God Love is [handwritten annotation]

Several times during the day, you might stop and ask yourself, *"What kind of people am I connecting with now?"* Ask yourself periodically, *"What do I really believe about this condition or situation?"* And think about it. Ask: *"What do I feel? Do I really want to do what these people are asking me? Why am I doing this?"* Start to examine your thoughts and feelings. Be honest with yourself. Find out what you are thinking and believing. Don't go on automatic pilot, living your life by routine: "This is the way I am, and this is what I do." Why do you do it? If it isn't a positive, nourishing experience, figure out where it came from. When did you first do it? You know what to do now. Connect to the Intelligence within you.

Stress Is Another Word for Fear

We talk a lot about stress these days. Everyone seems to be stressed out about something. Stress seems to be a buzzword and we use it to the point where I think it's a copout. "I'm so stressed," or "This is so stressful," or "All this stress, stress, stress."

Stress, to me, is a fearful reaction to life's constant changes. It is an excuse we use for not taking responsibility for our feelings. If we can equate the word "stress" with the word "fear," then we can begin to eliminate the need for fear in our lives.

The next time you think about how stressed you are, ask yourself what is scaring you. Ask: *"How am I overloading or burdening myself? Why am I giving my power away?"* Find out what you are doing to yourself that is creating this fear within you that keeps you from achieving inner harmony and peace.

Stress is not inner harmony. Inner harmony is being at peace with yourself. It's not possible to have stress and inner harmony at the same time. When you're at peace, you do things one at a time. You don't let things get to you. When you feel stressed, do something to release the fear, so you can move through life feeling safe. Don't use the word "stress" as a copout. Don't give a little word like "stress" a lot of power. Nothing has any power over you.

You Are Always Safe

Life is a series of doors closing and opening. We walk from room to room having different experiences. Many of us would like to close some doors on old negative patterns, old blocks, situations that are no longer nourishing or useful to ourselves. Many of us are in the process of opening new doors and finding wonderful new experiences.

I think that we come to this planet many, many times, and we come to learn different lessons. It's like coming to school. Before we incarnate at any particular time on the planet, we decide the lesson we are going to learn so that we can evolve spiritually. Once we choose our lesson, we choose all the circumstances and situations that will enable us to learn the lesson, including our parents, sexuality, place of birth, and race. If you've gotten this far in your life, believe me, you've made all the right choices.

As you go through life, it is essential to remind yourself that you are safe. It is only change. Trust your Higher Self to lead you and guide you in ways that are best for your spiritual growth. As Joseph Campbell once said, "Follow your bliss."

See yourself opening doors to joy, peace, healing, prosperity, and love; doors to understanding, compassion, forgiveness and freedom; doors to self-worth, self-esteem and self-love. You are eternal. You will go on forever from experience to experience. Even when you pass through the last doorway on this planet, it is not the end. It is the beginning of another new adventure.

Ultimately, you cannot force anyone to change. You can offer them a positive mental atmosphere where they have the possibility to change if they wish. However, you cannot do it for or to other people. Each person is here to work out his or her own lessons, and if you fix it for them, then they will eventually do it again because they haven't learned for themselves. They haven't worked out what they needed to do.

Love your sisters and brothers. Allow them to be who they are. Know that the truth is always within them, and they can change at any moment that they want.

Chapter 15

A World Where It's Safe to Love Each Other

We can either destroy the planet or we can heal it. Send some loving, healing energy to the planet every day. What we do with our minds makes a difference.

The planet is very much in a period of change and transition. We're going from an old order to a new order, and some people say it began with the Aquarian Age—at least the astrologers like to describe it in that way. To me, astrology, numerology, palmistry, and all those methods of psychic phenomena are merely ways of describing life. They explain life to us slightly differently.

So the astrologers say that we are moving out of the Piscean Age into the Aquarian Age. During the Piscean Age, we looked to other people to save us. We looked for other people to do it for us. In the Aquarian Age, which we are now entering, people are beginning to go within, acknowledging that they have the ability to save themselves.

Isn't it wonderfully liberating to change what we don't like? Actually, I'm not so sure that the planet is changing, as much as we are becoming more conscious and aware. Conditions that were brewing for a long time are coming to the surface, such as family dysfunction, child abuse, and our endangered planet.

As with everything else, first we must become aware in order to make changes. In the same way that we do our mental housecleaning so that we can change, we are doing the same thing with Mother Earth.

We are beginning to see our earth as a whole, living, breathing organism, an entity, a being unto itself. It breathes. It has a heartbeat. It takes care of its children. It provides everything here that we could possibly need. It's totally balanced. If you spend a day in the forest or somewhere in nature, you can see how all the systems on the planet work perfectly. It's set up to live out its existence in absolute, perfect equilibrium and harmony.

So here we are, great mankind who knows so much, and we are doing our very best to destroy the planet by disrupting this balance and harmony. Our greed gets in the way to an enormous extent. We think we know best, and through ignorance and greed we are destroying the living, breathing organism of which we are a part. If we destroy earth, where are we going to live?

I know that when I talk to people about caring more for the planet, they become overwhelmed by the problems we are encountering now. It seems that just one person doing something will not affect anything in the entire scheme of things. But that is not so. If everyone did a little it would wind up being a lot. You may not be able to see the effects right in front of you, but believe me, Mother Earth feels it collectively.

We have a little table set up to sell books at my aids support group. Recently we ran out of bags to put products in, so I thought I would start saving the bags I received when I was out shopping. At first, I thought, "Oh, you won't have that many bags by the end of the week," but boy, was I mistaken! I had bags coming out of my ears! One of my workers experienced the same thing. He said he had no idea how many bags a week he used until he started saving them. And when you put that in terms of Mother Earth, that's quite a few trees we're cutting down just to use for one or two hours, because we usually end up throwing the bags away. If you don't believe me, just try it for one week: save all the bags you receive and just be aware of how many you use.

Now I have a cloth shopping bag that I use and if I am shopping and have forgotten to bring it, I ask for a big bag and as I shop at other stores, I put my merchandise in one bag instead of collecting several. No one has ever looked at me twice for doing it. It just seems so sensible.

In Europe they have been using cloth shopping bags for a long time. A friend of mine from England visited and loved to go shopping at the supermarkets here because he wanted to carry the paper bags home. He thought they were very American and very chic. It may be a cute tradition, but the truth is we have to start thinking globally and consider the effects that these little traditions have on our environment.

American's particularly have a thing about the packaging of products. When I was in Mexico a few years ago, I visited a traditional market place and was fascinated by the unvarnished fruits and vegetables that were laid out. They certainly weren't as pretty as the ones we have in the states, but they looked natural and healthy to me, however some of the people I was with thought they looked terrible and unappealing.

In another part of the market there were open bins with powdered spices in it. Again it fascinated me because all the bins next to each other looked so bright and colorful. My friends said that they would never buy any spices from an open bin like that and I asked, "Why?" They said because it wasn't clean. When I asked why again, the answer came back that it was because it wasn't in a package. I had to laugh. Where did they think the spices were before they were put in a package? We have become so used to having things presented to us in a certain way that it's hard to accept it if we don't have all the frills and pretty packaging attached to it.

Let's be willing to see where we can make small adjustments for the sake of the environment. Even if all you do is buy a cloth shopping bag, or turn the water tap off while you brush your teeth, you have contributed a great deal by doing it.

At my office, we conserve as much as possible. There's a maintenance man in our building who picks up our recyclable copy paper every week and takes it to the recycling plant. We reuse padded envelopes. We use recycled paper in our books whenever possible, even though it costs a little more. Sometimes, it isn't possible to get, but we always ask for it anyway as we realize that if we continue to ask for it, eventually enough printers will have it available. It works that way in all areas of conservation. By creating a demand for something, we can help heal the planet in different ways as a collective power.

At home I am an organic gardener and make compost for the garden. Every piece of used vegetation goes into that compost pile. Not a lettuce leaf nor a leaf from a tree leaves my property. I believe in returning to the land what is taken away. I have a few friends who even save their vegetable trimmings for me. They put them into a bag in the freezer and when they visit they put their collection into my compost bin. What goes in as trash, comes out as rich earth filled with nourishment for plants. Because of my recycling practices, my garden produces lavishly for all my needs and is beautiful too.

Eat Nourishing Foods

Our planet is designed to give us every single thing we need to take care of ourselves. It has all the food we need. If we eat the foods of the planet, we're going to be healthy because it is part of the natural design. However, we, in our great intelligence, have designed foods such as Twinkies, and we wonder why our health isn't so good. A lot of us give lip service to diets. We say, "Yes, we know," as we reach for one sugar-filled treat after another. Two generations ago when Betty Crocker or Clarence Birdseye or whomever, came out with the first convenience-type food, we said, "Oh, isn't this wonderful!" Then came another and another and another, until generations later, there are people in this country who have never tasted real food. Everything is canned, processed, frozen, chemicalized, and, ultimately, microwaved.

I recently read that the young people in the military to-day do not have the healthy immune systems that youths had 20 years ago. If we don't give our body natural foods, which it needs to build and repair itself, how can we expect it to last a lifetime? Add to this: drugs, cigarettes, and alcohol abuse, a dose of self-hatred, and you have the perfect climate for dis-ease to flourish.

I had a very interesting experience recently. I took something called a "Responsible Driver's Course." It was filled with people over 55 years of age who were there ostensibly to get 3 to 10 percent off their auto insurance. I really found it fascinating that we spent the whole morning talking about illness—all the illnesses we could look forward to as we grow older. We talked about dis-eases of the eyes and everything that could go wrong with our ears and our hearts. When lunchtime came, 90 percent of these same people ran across the street to the nearest fast-food restaurant.

I thought to myself, we still don't get it, do we? One thousand people a day die from smoking. That's 365,000 people a year. I understand that over 500,000 people die from cancer each year. A million people die from heart attacks every year. A million people! Knowing this, why do we still run out to fast-food restaurants and pay so little attention to our bodies?

Healing Ourselves and Our Planet

Part of the catalyst for this transitional period is the crisis of aids. The aids crisis is showing how unloving and prejudiced we are toward one another. We treat people with aids with such little compassion. One of the things that I would really like to see happen on this planet, and I want to help create this, is a world where it is safe for us to love each other.

When we were little, we wanted to be loved for who we were, even if we were too skinny or too fat, too ugly, or too shy. We come to this planet to learn unconditional love—first to have it for ourselves, and then to give the same unconditional love to other people. We need to get rid of this idea of *them and us*. There is no *them and us*; there is only us. There are no groups that are expendable or *less than*.

Every one of us has a list of *those* people *over there*. We can't really be spiritual as long as there is one person *over there*. Many of us grew up in families where prejudice was normal and natural. This group or that group was not good enough. In order to make ourselves feel better, we would put the other group down. However, as long as we are saying that someone else isn't good enough, what we're really reflecting is that *we're* not good enough. Remember, we're all mirrors of each other.

I remember when I was invited to *The Oprah Winfrey Show*. I appeared on TV with five people with aids who were doing quite well. The six of us had met the evening before for dinner, and it was such an incredibly powerful gathering. When we sat down to have dinner, the energy was extraordinary. I started to cry because this was something I had been striving for for several years— to get a positive message out to the American public that there is hope. These people were healing themselves, and it wasn't easy. The medical community told them that they were going to die. They had to experiment with many different methods by trial and error, and they were willing to expand and go beyond their own limitations.

We taped the next day, and it was a beautiful show. I was pleased that women with aids were also represented on the show. I wanted Middle America to open their hearts and to realize that aids doesn't affect a group that they don't care about. It affects everybody. When I came out, Oprah said to me off-camera, "Louise, Louise, Louise," and came up to me and gave me a big hug.

I believe we relayed the message of hope that day. I've heard Dr. Bernie Siegel say that there is someone who has healed his or herself of every form of cancer. So there is always hope, and hope gives us possibilities. There is something to work towards instead of throwing up our hands and saying there's nothing that can be done.

The aids virus is just doing its thing—being what it is. It breaks my heart to realize that there will be more and more heterosexual people who are going to die from aids because the government and the medical profession are not moving fast enough. As long as aids is perceived as a "gay" dis-ease, it will not receive the attention it urgently needs, so how many "straight" people will have to die before it's considered a legitimate illness?

I think the faster we all put away our prejudices and work for a positive solution to this crisis, the faster the whole planet will heal. However, we can't heal the planet if we allow people to suffer. To me, aids is very much a part of the pollution of the planet. Do you realize that dolphins off the coast of California are dying of immune deficiency dis-eases? I don't believe it's because of their sexual practices. We've been polluting our lands so that a lot of the vegetation is unfit to eat. We are killing the fish in our waters. We are polluting our air, so now there is acid rain and a hole in the ozone layer. And we continue polluting our bodies.

Aids is a terrible, terrible dis-ease, yet the numbers of people who are dying from aids are far fewer than those who are dying from cancer, smoking, and heart dis-ease. We search for ever-more potent poisons to kill the dis-eases we create, yet we don't want to change our lifestyles and diets. We either want some drug to suppress our illness, or we want to surgically remove it, rather than heal it. The more we suppress, the more that problems manifest in other ways. It's even more incredible to learn that medicine and surgery only take care of 10 percent of all dis-ease. That's right. Even with all the money we spend on chemicals, radiation, and surgery, they only help 10 percent of our dis-eases!

I read an article that said that the dis-eases in the next century will be caused by new strains of bacteria that will affect our weakened immune systems. These bacteria strains have begun to mutate, so that the drugs we have now will have no effect upon them. Obviously, the more we build up our immune systems, the quicker we are going to heal ourselves and the planet. And I'm not only referring to our physical immune systems; I mean our mental and emotional immune systems as well.

To me, healing and curing bring about two different results. I think healing needs to be a team effort. If you expect your doctor to fix you, he or she may take care of the symptoms; however, that doesn't heal the problem. Healing is making yourself whole. To be healed, you must be a part of the team, you and your doctor or health care professional. There are many holistic M.D.'s who not only treat you physically, but who see you as a whole person.

We have been living with erroneous belief systems, not only individual ones, but societal ones as well. There are people who say that earaches run in their family. Others believe that when they go out in the rain, they catch cold, or they get three colds every winter. Or, when someone catches a cold in the office, everyone gets a cold because it's contagious. "Contagious" is an idea, and the idea is contagious.

A lot of people talk about dis-ease being hereditary. I don't think that's necessarily so. I think that what we pick up are the mental patterns of our parents. Children are very aware. They begin to imitate their parents, even their illnesses. If a father tightens his colon every time he feels angry, the child picks up on that. It's no wonder that

Memorize this

when the father gets colitis years later, the child get colitis, too. Everyone knows that cancer is not contagious, yet why does it run in families? Because the patterns of resentment run in families. Resentment builds and builds until finally there is cancer.

We must allow ourselves to be aware of everything so that we can make conscious, intelligent choices. Some things may horrify us (which is part of the awakening process), but then we can do something about them. Everything in the Universe from child abuse and aids, to the homeless situation and starvation, needs our love. A tiny child who is loved and appreciated will become a strong, self-assured adult. The planet, which has everything here for us and all of life, if we allow it to be itself, will take care of us always. Let's not think about our past limitations.

Let's open ourselves to the potential of this incredible decade. We can make these final 10 years of the century a time of healing. We have the Power within us to clean up—clean our bodies, our emotions, and all the various messes we have made. We can look around and see what needs care. The way each of us chooses to live will have a tremendous impact on our future and on our world.

For the Highest Good of All

You can take this time to apply your personal growth methods to the entire planet. If you just do things for the planet and not for yourself, then you're not in balance. If you only work for yourself and stop there, then that's not balanced either.

So let's see how we can begin to balance ourselves *and* the environment. We know that our thoughts shape and create our lives. We don't always live the philosophy totally; nonetheless, we've accepted the basic premise. If we want to change our immediate world, we must change our thinking. If we want to change the greater world around us, we need to change our thinking about it, not viewing it as *them and us.*

If all the effort you put out in complaining about what's wrong with the world is applied to positive affirmations and visualizations of the world, you could begin to turn things around. Remember, every time you use your mind, you are connecting to like-minded people. If you inflict judgment, criticism, and prejudice on others, you are connecting to all the other people who are doing the same. However, if you are meditating, visualizing peace, loving yourself, and loving the planet, you are connecting with these kinds of people. You could be at home, bed-ridden, and still help to heal the planet by the way you use your mind—by practicing inner peace. I heard Robert Schuller of the United Nations once say, *"The human species needs to know that we deserve to have peace."* How true those words are.

If we can make our young people aware of what is happening in the world and give them options as to what they can do about it, then we can really begin to see a shift in consciousness. Teaching our children early about conservation efforts is one way to reassure them that important work is being done. Even though some adults still won't take responsibility for what is going on in the world around them, we can assure our children that more and more people throughout the world are becoming aware of the long-term effects of global pollution and are striving to change the situation. Becoming involved as a family in an ecological foundation such as *Greenpeace* or *Earthsave* is wonderful, as it is never too soon to impress upon children that we all have to accept responsibility for the good of our planet.

I recommend that you read John Robbins' book, *Diet For A New America*. I find it so interesting that John Robbins, heir to the Baskin-Robbins ice cream business, is doing his best to help create a holistic and peaceful planet. It's wonderful to know that some of the children of people who exploit the health of the nation turn around and do things to help the planet.

Volunteer groups are also helping to take over where the government is falling short. If the government won't help heal our environment, we can't sit around and wait. We have to get together on a grass roots level and take care of it. We can all do our part. Start to find out where you can help. Volunteer where you can. Give one hour a month if you can't do anything else.

We are definitely on the cutting edge of the forces that are going to help heal this planet. We are at a point right now where we can all go down the tubes or we can heal the planet. It isn't up to *them*, it's up to us, individually and collectively.

I see more opportunities for a blending of the scientific technologies of the past and the future with the spiritual truths of yesterday, today, and tomorrow. It is time that these elements come together. By understanding that acts of violence come from a person who is a traumatized child, we could combine our knowledge and technologies to help them change. We don't perpetuate violence by starting wars or throwing people in prisons and forgetting them. Instead, we encourage self-awareness, self-esteem, and self-love. The tools for transformation are available; we just have to use them.

Lazaris has a wonderful exercise that I would like to share with you. Pick a spot on the planet. It could be anywhere—very far away or just around the corner—some place on the planet that you would like to help heal. Envision that place as peaceful, with people well fed and clothed and living in safety and peace. Take a moment every day and envision it.

Put your love to work to help heal the planet. You are important. By sharing your love and all the magnificent gifts within you will begin to change the energy on this beautiful, blue-green, fragile planet that we call our home.

And so it is!

Afterword

I remember when I couldn't sing very well at all. I still don't sing very well, but I am much more brave. I lead people in song at the end of my workshops and support groups. Perhaps one day, I will take some lessons and learn; however, I haven't gotten around to it yet.

At one event I began to lead everyone in song, and the man in charge of the sound system turned off my microphone. Joseph Vattimo, my assistant, said, "What are you doing?" The other man said, "She's singing off key!" It was so terribly embarrassing. Now, it really doesn't matter anymore. I just sing my heart out, and it seems to open up just a little bit more.

I've had some extraordinary experiences in my life, and the one that has opened my heart on a very deep level has been working with people with aids. I can hug people now who, three years ago, I couldn't even look at. I've gone beyond a lot of my own personal limitations. In reward for that, I have found so much love—wherever I go, people give me tremendous amounts of love.

In October 1987, Joseph and I went to Washington, D.C., to march for governmental help for aids. I don't know how many are aware of the *aids quilt*. It's rather incredible. Many, many people from around the country got together and made quilt patches to commemorate someone who has died from aids. These patches are made with so much love and put together with patches from all over the world to make an enormous quilt.

When we were in Washington, the patches were put into sections and displayed between the Washington and Lincoln monuments. At six o'clock in the morning, we began to read the names of the people on the quilt. As we did, people would unfold the patch and put it in place next to the others. It was a very emotional time, as you can imagine. People were crying everywhere.

I was standing with my list, waiting to read, when I felt this tap on my shoulder. I could hear someone say, "Could I ask you a question, please?" I turned around, and the young man standing behind me looked at the badge with my name on it, and shouted, "Louise Hay! Oh my God," and he went into absolute hysteria and flung himself in my arms. We held each other, and he just sobbed and sobbed. Finally, when he could contain himself, he told me that his lover had read my book many times, and when he was about to leave the planet, his lover asked him to read a treatment from my book. He read it slowly, as his lover read the lines with him. The very last words his lover said were, "All is well," and he died.

So here I was, right in front of him. He was extremely touched. When he could compose himself enough, I said, "But what did you want to ask me?" It seemed that he had not been able to complete his lover's patch on time, and he wanted me to add his lover's name to my list. He just happened to pick me. I remember this moment very well, because it showed me that life is really simple and the things that are important are also simple.

I want to share a quote with you from Emmett Fox. If you don't know Emmett Fox, he was a very popular teacher in the '40s, '50s, and early '60s and one of the clearest teachers I know. He has written some beautiful books, and these are some of my favorite words of his:

> *"There is no difficulty that enough love will not conquer. There is no disease that enough love will not heal. No door that enough love will not open. No gulf that enough love will not bridge. No wall that enough love will not throw down. And no sin that enough love will not redeem. It makes no difference how deeply seated may be the trouble. How hopeless the outlook. How muddled the tangle. How great the mistake. A sufficient realization of love will dissolve it all. And if you could love enough you would be the happiest and most powerful person in the world."*

It's true, you know. It sounds wonderful and it is true. What do you need to do to get to that space where you could be the happiest and most powerful person in the world? I think inner space travel is just beginning. We are just beginning to learn about the Power that we have inside us. We're not going to find it if we contract. The more we can open to ourselves, the more we are going to find the Universal energies available to assist us. There are incredible accomplishments that we are capable of.

Take a few breaths. Open your chest and give your heart room to expand. Keep practicing, and sooner or later the barriers will begin to drop. Today is your beginning point.

I love you,

Laurie L. Nay

Meditations for Personal and Planetary Healing

Acknowledge yourself for being cen-
tered when there is incredible chaos
around you. Acknowledge yourself for
being courageous and for doing so much
more than you thought you could.

The healing work we do at the end of our workshops and support groups is very powerful. We usually break into groups of three and do a form of laying-on-of-hands for each other. It is a wonderful way to accept energy and also share energy with many people who are reluctant in one way or another to ask for help. Often, profound experiences occur.

I would like to share some of the meditations we do at our healing circles. It would be wonderful if we all did them on an ongoing basis either by ourselves or in groups.

Touching Your Inner Child

See your inner child in any way that you can and notice how it looks and feels. Comfort your child. Apologize to

217

it. Tell it how sorry you are for forsaking it. You have been away for so long, and you are now willing to make it up. Promise this little child that you will never ever leave her or him again. Anytime it wants, it can reach out and touch you, and you will be there. If it is scared, you will hold it. If it is angry, it is okay to express the anger. Tell it you love it very much.

You have the power to help create the kind of world that you want you and your child to live in. You have the power of your mind and your thoughts. See yourself creating a wonderful world. See your child relaxed and safe, peaceful, laughing, happy, playing with friends. Running free. Touching a flower. Hugging a tree. Picking an apple from the tree, and eating it with delight. Playing with a puppy or a kitten. Swinging high above the trees. Laughing with joy and running up to you and giving you a big hug.

See the two of you healthy and living in a beautiful, safe place. Having wonderful relationships with your parents, friends and co-workers. Being greeted with joy wherever you go. Having a special kind of love. See where you want to live and what you want to work at. And see yourselves as healthy. Very healthy. Joyous. And free. And so it is.

A Healthy World

Envision the world as a great place to live in. See all the sick being made well and the homeless being cared for. See dis-ease become a thing of the past, and all the hospitals now apartment buildings. See prison inmates being taught how to love themselves and being released as responsible citizens. See churches remove sin and guilt from their teachings. See governments really taking care of people.

Go outside and feel the clean rain falling. As the rain stops, see a beautiful rainbow appear. Notice the sun shining, and the air is clean and clear. Smell its freshness. See the water glisten and sparkle in our rivers, streams, and lakes. And notice the lush vegetation. Forests filled with trees. Flowers, fruits, and vegetables abundant and available everywhere. See people being healed of dis-ease, so that illness becomes a memory.

Go to other countries and see peace and plenty for all. See harmony between all people as we lay down our guns. Judgment, criticism, and prejudice become archaic and fade away. See borders crumbling and separateness disappearing. See all of us becoming one. See our Mother Earth, the planet, healed and whole.

You are creating this new world now, just by using your mind to envision a new world. You are powerful. You are important, and you do count. Live your vision. Go out and do what you can to make this vision come true. God bless us all. And so it is.

Your Healing Light

Look deep within the center of your heart and find that tiny little pinpoint of brilliantly colored light. It is such a beautiful color. It is the very center of your love and healing energy. Watch the little pinpoint of light begin to pulsate, and as it pulsates, it grows until it fills your heart. See this light move through your body from the top of your head to the tip of your toes and the tip of your fingers. You are absolutely glowing with this beautiful colored light. It is your love and your healing energy. Let your whole body vibrate with this light. You can say to yourself, *"With every breath I take, I am getting healthier and healthier."*

Feel this light cleansing your body of dis-ease and allowing normal health to return to you. Let this light begin to radiate out from you in all directions, touching the people around you. Let your healing energy touch everyone whom you know who needs it. What a privilege it is to share your love and light and healing energy with those who are in need of healing. Let your light move into hospitals and nursing homes and orphanages and prisons, mental hospitals, and other institutions of despair. Let it bring hope and enlightenment and peace.

Let it move into every home in the city in which you live where there is pain and suffering. Let your love and light and healing energy bring comfort to those in need. Let it move into the churches and soften the hearts of those involved, so that they truly operate with unconditional love. Let the beautiful light that comes from your heart move into the Capitol and government buildings, bringing enlightenment and the message of truth. Let it move into every capital in every government. Select one place on the planet as a place that you would like to help heal. Concentrate your light on that place. It may be very far away or it may be around the corner. Concentrate your love and light and your healing energy on this place and see it come into balance and harmony. See it whole. Take a moment every day to send your love and light and healing energy to this particular place on the planet. We are the people. We are the children. We are the world. We are the future. What we give out comes back to us multiplied. And so it is.

Receiving Prosperity

Let's realize some positive qualities for ourselves. We are open and receptive to wonderful new ideas. We allow prosperity to enter into our lives on a level that it has never entered before. We deserve the best. We are willing to accept the best. Our income is constantly increasing. We move away from poverty thinking into prosperity thinking. We love ourselves. We rejoice in who we are and we know that life is here for us and will supply us with everything that we need. We move from success to success, from joy to joy, and from abundance to abundance. We are one with the Power that created us. We express for ourselves the greatness that we are. We are divine, magnificent expressions of Life, and we are open and receptive to all good. And so it is.

Welcome the Child

Put your hand over your heart. Close your eyes. Allow yourself not only to see your inner child but to be that child. Let your own voice speak for your parents as they welcome you into the world and into their lives. Hear them say:

We're so glad you came. We've been waiting for you. We wanted you so much to be part of our family. You're so important to us. We're so glad you are a little boy. We're so glad you are a little girl. We love your uniqueness and your specialness. The family wouldn't be the same without you. We love you. We want to hold you. We want to help you grow up to be all that you can be. You don't have to be like us. You can be yourself. You're so beautiful. You're so bright. You're so creative. It gives us such pleasure to have you here. We love you more than anything in the whole world. We thank you for choosing our family. We know you're blessed. You have blessed us by coming. We love you. We really love you.

Let your little child make these words true for it. Be aware that every day you can hold yourself and say these words. You can look in the mirror and say these words. You can hold a friend and say these words.

Tell yourself all the things you wanted your parents to tell you. Your little child needs to feel wanted and loved. Give that to your child. No matter how old you are or how sick, or how scared, your little child needs to be wanted and loved. Keep telling your child, "I want you and I love you." It is the truth for you. The Universe wants you here, and that's why you are here. You've always been loved and will always be loved throughout eternity. You can live happily ever after. And so it is.

Love is Healing

Love is the most powerful healing force there is. I open myself to love. I am willing to love and be loved. I see myself prosper. I see myself healthy. I see myself creatively fulfilled. I live in peace and safety.

Send everyone you know thoughts of comfort and acceptance and support and love. Be aware that as you send these thoughts out, you also receive them back.

Envelop your family in a circle of love, whether they are living or not. Include your friends, the people at work, and everyone from your past, and all the people you would like to forgive, but don't know how.

Send love to everyone with aids and cancer, and to the friends and lovers, hospice workers, doctors, nurses, alternative therapists, and caretakers. Let's see an end to aids and cancer. In your mind's eye, see a headline that reads, "Cure for cancer found. Cure for aids found."

Put yourself in this circle of love. Forgive yourself. Affirm that you have wonderful, harmonious relationships with your parents, where there is mutual respect and caring on both sides.

Let the circle of love envelop the entire planet, and let your heart open so you can find that space within you where there is unconditional love. See everyone living with dignity and in peace and joy.

You are worth loving. You are beautiful. You are powerful. You open yourself to all good. And so it is.

We Are Free to be Ourselves

In order to be whole, we must accept all of ourselves. So let your heart open and make plenty of room in there for all the parts of yourself. The parts you are proud of and the part that embarrass you. The parts you reject and the parts you love. They are all of you. You are beautiful. We all are. When your heart is full of love for yourself, then you have so much to share with others.

Let this love now fill your room and permeate out to all the people that you know. Put the people you want in the center of your room so that they can receive the love from your overflowing heart. From your child to theirs. Now see all the children in all the people dancing as children dance, skipping and shouting and turning somersaults and cartwheels, filled with exuberant joy. Expressing all the best of the child within.

Let your child go and play with the other children. Let your child dance. Let your child feel safe and free. Let your child be all that it ever wanted to be. You are perfect, whole, and complete, and all is well in your wonderful world. And so it is.

Sharing Healing Energy

Shake your hands and then rub them together. Then share the energy in your hands with the beautiful being before you. It is such an honor and privilege to share healing energy with another human being. It is such a simple thing to do.

Whenever you are with friends, you can spend a little time sharing healing energy. We need to give to each other and receive from each other in simple, meaningful ways. The touch that says *I care*. We may not be able to fix anything, but we care. *I'm here for you and I love you.* Together we can find the answers.

All dis-ease comes to an end. All crises come to an end. Feel the healing energies. Let that energy, that intelligence, that knowledge be awakened in us. We deserve to heal. We deserve to be whole. We deserve to know and love who we are. Divine love has always met and always will meet every human need. And so it is.

A Circle of Love

See yourself standing in a very safe space. Release your burdens and pains and fears. Old negative addictions and patterns. See them falling away from you. Then see yourself standing in your safe place with your arms wide open, saying "I am open and receptive to_____." Declaring for yourself what it is you want. Not what you don't want, but what you do want. And know that it is possible. See yourself whole and healthy. At peace. See yourself filled with love.

All we need is one idea to change our lives. On this planet we can be in a circle of hate or we can be in a circle of love and healing. I choose to be in a circle of love. I realize that everyone wants the same things that I want.

We want to express ourselves creatively in ways that are fulfilling. We want to be peaceful and safe.

And in this space, feel your connection with other people in the world. Let the love in you go from heart to heart. And as your love goes out, know that it comes back to you multiplied. *"I send comforting thoughts to everyone and know that these thoughts are returning to me."* See the world becoming an incredible circle of light. And so it is.

You Deserve Love

We don't have to believe everything. In the perfect time-space sequence, that which you need will rise to the surface. Each one of us has the ability to love ourselves more. Each one of us deserves to be loved. We deserve to live well, to be healthy, to be loved and loving, to prosper, and the little child deserves to grow up to have a wonderful, wonderful life.

See yourself surrounded by love. See yourself happy and healthy and whole. See yourself as you would like your life to be. Put in all the details. Know that you deserve it. Then take the love from your heart and let it begin to flow, filling your body with healing energies.

Let your love begin to flow around the room and around your home until you are in an absolutely enormous circle of love. Feel the love circulating, so as it goes out from you, it returns to you. The most powerful healing force is love. Let it circulate over and over again. Let it wash through your body. You are love. And so it is.

A New Decade

See a new door opening to a decade of great healing. Healing that we have not understood in the past. We are in the process of learning the incredible abilities that we have within ourselves. And we are learning to get in touch with those parts of ourselves that have the answers and are there to lead us and guide us in ways that are for our highest good.

So let's see this new door opening wide and ourselves stepping through it to find healing in many, many different forms. For healing means different things to different people. Many of us have bodies that need healing. Some of us have hearts that need healing, or minds that need healing. So we are open and receptive to the healing that we each need individually. We open the door wide for personal growth, and we move through this doorway, knowing we are safe. It is only change. And so it is.

Spirit Am I

We are the only ones who can save the world. As we band together with a common cause, we find the answers. We must always remember that there is a part of us that is far more than our bodies, far more than our personalities, far more than our dis-eases, and more than our past. There is a part of us that is more than our relationships. The very central core of us is pure spirit. Eternal. Always has been and always will be.

We are here to love ourselves. And to love each other.

By doing this, we will find the answers so that we can heal ourselves and the planet. We are going through extraordinary times. All sorts of things are changing. We may not even know the depth of the problems. Yet, we are swimming as best as we can. This, too, shall pass, and we will find solutions.

We are spirit. And we are free. We connect on a spiritual level, for we know that level can never be taken from us. And on the level of spirit, we are all one. We are free. And so it is.

A World That Is Safe

You might like to hold a hand on either side of you. We've touched on many things, and each of us has something we relate to. We've talked about negative things and positive things. We've talked about fears and frustrations, and how scary it is to go up to somebody and just say, "Hello." Many of us still do not trust ourselves to take care of ourselves. And we feel lost and lonely.

Yet we have been working on ourselves for some time and have noticed that our lives are changing. Lots of problems in the past aren't problems anymore. It doesn't change overnight, but if we are persistent and consistent, positive things do happen.

So let's share the energy we have and the love we have with people on either side of us. Know that as we give from our hearts, we are also receiving from other hearts. Let's open our hearts so that we can take in everyone in the room with love, support, and caring. Let's move that love to people in the street who have no homes and no place to go. Let's share our love with those who are angry, frightened or in pain. Every person. And all those in denial. Those who are in the process of leaving the planet, and those who have already left.

Let's share our love with everybody, whether they accept it or not. There is no way we can be hurt if our love is rejected. Let's hold the entire planet in our hearts, the animals, fish, the birds, the vegetation, and all the people. All the people we are angry at, or frustrated with. Those who are not doing it our way, and those who are expressing so-called evil. Let's take them into our hearts, too. So that out of the feeling of safety, they can begin to recognize who they really are.

See peace breaking out all over the planet. Know that you are contributing to peace right now. Rejoice that you have the ability to do something. You are a beautiful, person. Acknowledge yourself for how wonderful you are. Know that it is the truth for you. And so it is.

Loving All The Parts of Ourselves

I would like you to go back in time to when you were five years old and see yourself as clearly as you can. Look at that little child, and with your arms outstretched, say to that child: *"I am your future and I have come to love you."* Embrace the child and bring it forward with you to present time. Now both of you stand in front of a mirror so you can look at each other with love.

You see that there are a few parts of you that are missing. Once again go back in time to the moment you were first born. You were wet and felt the cold air on your body. You had just come through a difficult journey. The lights were bright, and the umbilical cord was still attached, and you were scared. Yet here you were ready to start life on this planet. Love the little baby.

Move to the time when you were just learning to walk. You stood up and fell down and stood up and fell down once again. Suddenly you took your first step, and then another step and another. You were so proud of yourself. Love the little child.

Move forward to your first day of school. You didn't want to leave your mother. You were brave to step across the threshold of a new period of time in your life. You did the very best you could with the whole situation. Love the little child.

Now you are ten years old. You remember what was going on. It may have been wonderful or frightful. You were doing the very best to survive. Love the ten-year-old child.

Go forward to when you just entered puberty and were a teenager. It may have been exciting because you were finally growing up. It may have been frightening because there was a lot of peer pressure to look right and act the right way. You handled it the best you could. Love the teenager.

Now you are graduating high school. You knew more than your parents. You were ready to begin your life now the way you wanted. You were brave and scared all at the same time. Love that young adult.

Now remember your first day at work. The first time

you earned money and you were so proud. You wanted
to do well. There was so much to learn. You did the best
you knew how. Love that person.

Think of another milestone in your life. A marriage.
Your own child. A new home. It may have been a dread-
ful experience or a wonderful one. Somehow you handled
it. You survived in the best way you could. Love the person you are.

Now bring all these parts of yourself forward, and
stand in front of the mirror so you can look at each of
them with love. Coming towards you is yet another part.
Your future stands with arms outstretched and says, *"I
am here to love you."* And so it is.

Feel Your Power

Feel your power. Feel the power of your breath. Feel the
power of your sound. Feel the power of your love. Feel
the power of your forgiveness. Feel the power of your
willingness to change. Feel your power. You are beautiful. You are a divine, magnificent being. You deserve all
good, not just some, but *all* good. Feel your power. Be
at peace with it, for you are safe. Welcome this new day
with open arms and with love. And so it is.

The Light Has Come

Sit opposite your partner and hold your partner's hands.
Look into each other's eyes. Take a nice deep breath and

release any fear that you may have. Take another deep breath and release your judgment and allow yourself to be with this person. What you see in them is a reflection of you, a reflection of what is in you.

It's all right. We are all one. We breathe the same air. We drink the same water. We eat the foods of the earth. We have the same desires and needs. We all want to be healthy. We all want to love and be loved. We all want to live comfortably and peacefully, and we all want to prosper. We all want to live our lives with fulfillment.

Allow yourself to look at this person with love, and be willing to receive the love back. Know that you are safe. As you look at your partners, affirm for them the perfect health. Affirm for them loving relationships, so that they are surrounded by loving people wherever they may be. Affirm for them prosperity so that they live comfortably. Affirm for them comfort and safety and know that what you give out returns to you multiplied. So affirm the very best of everything, and know that they deserve it and see them willing to accept it. And so it is.

Self-Help Resources

The following list of resources can be used for more information about recovery options available for addictions or problems related to dysfunctional families. The addresses and telephone numbers listed are for the national headquarters; look in your local yellow pages under "Community Services" for resources closer to your area.

In addition to the following groups, other self-help organizations may be available in your area to assist your healing and recovery for particular life crises not listed here. Consult your telephone directory, call a counseling center or help line near, or write or call:

National Self-Help
Clearinghouse
33 West 42nd Street
New York, NY 10036
212-840-1259

Al-Anon Family Headquarters
1372 Broadway, 7th Floor
New York, NY 10018
800-245-4656

Alcoholics Anonymous (AA)
General Service Office
468 Park Avenue South
New York, NY 10016
212-686-1100

and
National Clearinghouse for Alcohol Information (NCALI)
P.O. Box 234
Rockville, MD 20852
301-468-2600

and
National Council on Alcoholism (NCA)
12 West 21st Street
New York, NY 10010
212-206-6770

and
National Institute on Alcohol Abuse and Alcoholism (NIAAA)
Parklawn Building
5600 Fishers Lane
Rockville, MD 20852
301-468-2600

American Anorexia/Bulimia Assn., Inc.
133 Cedar Lane
Teaneck, NJ 07666
201-836-1800

Children of Alcoholics Foundation
200 Park Avenue
31st Street
New York, NY 10166
212-949-1404

and
National Assn. of Children of Alcoholics (NACOA)
31706 Coast Highway
South Laguna, CA 92677
714-499-3889

Cocaine Anonymous
National Office
P.O. Box 1367
Culver City, CA 90232
213-559-5833

and
National Cocaine-Abuse Hotline
800-COCAINE (262-2463)

Gamblers Anonymous
National Council on Compulsive Gambling
444 West 56th St., Room 3207S
New York, NY 10019
212-765-3833

Incest Survivors Resource Network, Int'l, Inc.
P.O. Box 911
Hicksville, NY 11802
516-935-3031

and
Survivors of Incest Gaining Health (SIGH)
20 West Adams, Suite 2015
Chicago, IL 60606

Narcotics Anonymous (NA)
World Service Office
P.O. Box 9999
Van Nuys, CA 91409
818-780-3951

and

National Institute of Drug
Abuse (NIDA)
Parklawn Building
5600 Fishers Lane
Rockville, MD 20852
301-443-6245
(for information)
800-662-4357 (for help)

National Child Abuse Hotline
Childhelp USA
P.O. Box 630
Hollywood, CA 90028
800-422-4453 (4-A-CHILD)

and

National Committee for
Prevention of Child Abuse
322 S. Michigan Ave., Ste. 950
Chicago, IL 60604
312-663-3520

Overeaters Anonymous
National Office
4025 Spencer St., Ste. 203
Torrance, CA 90504
213-542-8363

Parents Anonymous
National Office
6733 S. Sepulveda Blvd.
Ste. 270
Los Angeles, CA 90045
800-421-0353

National Rape Information
Clearinghouse*
National Center for Prevention
and Control of Rape
Parklawn Building
5600 Fishers Lane
Rockville, MD 20857

and

National Coalition Against
Sexual Assault
c/o Austin Rape Crisis Center
P.O. Box 7156
Austin, TX 78713
512-440-7273

Students Against Suicide
P.O. Box 115
South Laguna, CA 92677
714-496-4566

*Also, contact your local
rape crisis center in the event
of an occurence.

Suggested Reading

Bradshaw: On The Family by John Bradshaw, Health Communications, Inc., 1988

Co-dependent No More by Melodie Beattie, Harper and Row, 1987

A Course In Miracles, Foundation for Inner Peace, 1975

Creative Visualization by Shakti Gawain, Whatever Publishing, 1978

Diet For A New America by John Robbins, Stillpoint Press, 1987

Emmanuel's Book compiled by Pat Rodegast and Judith Stanton, Bantam Books, 1985

Expectations And Possibilities by Joe Batten, Hay House, Inc., 1990

Feel The Fear And Do It Anyway by Susan Jeffers, Ph.D., Ballantine Books, 1987

50 Simple Things You Can Do To Save The Earth by The Earth Works Group, Earthworks Press, 1989

Fit For Life by Harvey and Marilyn Diamond, Warner Books, Inc., 1985

Getting Well Again by Carl Simonton, M.D., Bantam Books, 1980

Healing the Shame That Binds You by John Bradshaw, Health Communications, Inc., 1988

Homecoming: Reclaiming and Championing Your Inner Child by John Bradshaw, Bantam Books, 1990

I Come As A Brother by Bartholomew, High Mesa Press, 1986

The Knight in Rusty Armor by Robert Fisher, Wilshire Book Company, 1987

LifeGoals: Setting and Achieving Goals to Chart the Course of Your Life by Amy E. Dean, Hay House, 1991

Listening by Lee Coit, Las Brisas Retreat Center, 1985

Love Is Letting Go Of Fear by Gerald Jampolsky, M.D., Celestial Arts, 1979

Love, Medicine & Miracles by Bernie S. Siegel, M.D., Random House, 1986

Love Your Disease by John Harrison, M.D., Hay House, Inc., 1989

Out Of Darkness Into The Light by Gerald Jampolsky, M.D., Bantam Books, 1989

Miracles by Stuart Wilde, White Dove International, Inc., 1983

The Picture Of Health by Lucia Capacchione, Hay House, Inc., 1990

The Power Of Your Other Hand by Lucia Capacchione, Newcastle Publishing, 1988

The Power of Your Subconscious Mind by Joseph Murphy, Bantam Books, 1982

Power Through Constructive Thinking by Emmett Fox, Harper & Row, 1968

A New Design For Living by Ernest Holmes and Willis H. Kinnear, Prentice Hall, 1987

Re-Creating Your Self by Christopher Stone, Hay House, Inc., 1990

Return To The Garden by Shakti Gawain, New World Library, 1989

The Sacred Journey: You And Your Higher Self by Lazaris, Concept: Synergy Publishing, 1987

The Science of Mind by Ernest Holmes, G.P. Putnam's Sons, 1938

Self-Parenting by John Pollard III, Generic Human Studies Publishing, 1987

This Thing Called You by Ernest Holmes, G.P. Putnam's Sons, 1948

Unlimited Power by Anthony Robbins, Fawcett Columbine, 1986

Your Heart • Your Planet by Harvey Diamond, Hay House, Inc., 1990

When 9 To 5 Isn't Enough by Marcia A. Perkins-Reed, Hay House, Inc., 1990